THE NEWS MAKERS

BEHIND THE CAMERAS WITH CANADA'S TOP TV JOURNALISTS

EDITED BY LINDA FRUM

KEY PORTER BOOKS

Canadian Cataloguing in Publication Data
Main entry under title:
Newsmakers

ISBN 1-55013-168-0

1. Journalists — Canada —Anecdotes.   2. Journalism — Canada.   I. Frum, Linda, 1963-

PN4912.M33 1990   070.92'2   C89-094084-3

Key Porter Books Limited
70 The Esplanade
Toronto, Ontario
Canada M5E 1R2

Typesetting: Computer Composition of Canada Inc.

Printed and bound in Canada

90 91 92 93 94 95 6 5 4 3 2 1

CONTENTS

Editor's Note   v

Introduction   vii

What Is News?   1

Get the Story!   39

Close Encounters   81

Perks, Perils, and Pointers   113

Covering the Wars   145

The Home Front   185

Jean-Guy Nault: A Tribute   213

The Contributors   217

EDITOR'S NOTE

Prying personal stories out of Canada's leading television journalists is not easy. The stumbling block is not their discretion or good taste, but the "Code of the Road," which demands that all details of a journalist's personal doings abroad are kept secret. As one reporter explained: "Travelling on assignment is a very stressful experience. Four people, selected at random, are required to spend twenty-four hours a day together. They rely heavily on the telling of yarns to breach the basic barriers to coexistence. Naturally, the best yarns are the most scandalous, so there must be a guarantee that the content of the stories will remain private. Hence, the Code of the Road: Anything that happens on the road may be discussed only on the road among other people who are on the road."

Why would so many Canadian journalists simultaneously break the Code? For a friend, cameraman Jean-Guy Nault, one of the most talented professionals in the business. Nault is loved by all those who have worked with him, as much for his sunny disposition as for his extraordinary skill. He began his career with CJOH in Ottawa and went on to CTV, Global, and finally to CBC and *The Journal*. Because of his gifts as a cameraman, he was regularly chosen for demanding shoots, but it is his good nature and charm that make him the sort of person you would want to spend two weeks with on the road.

In 1985, while working in St. Andrew's-by-the-Sea on the "tainted tuna" story, Guy fell down some stairs and broke his neck. While he and his family put their lives and careers back together, his friends looked for a way to tell him how many people cared and wished him well. The result is this book, all royalties from which go to Guy.

Gordon Henderson has written a tribute to his friend Guy, and Canada's television journalists contributed their time, their recollections, and their affection. I am grateful to all those who allowed me to interview them, providing much more material than could be contained between these covers. Not all the journalists interviewed are represented in the finished book, but their affection for Jean-Guy, their spirit, and their goodwill is its real text.

This book is the result of the collaborative efforts of dozens of people. Altogether, over 70 newspeople agreed to be interviewed for these pages, and, as editor, I am truly appreciative of all those who contributed so graciously and eagerly. Among them were Bill Cameron, whose energy and enthusiasm got the project off the ground. The CBC's Ruth Ellen Soles, Brian Ekman, and Sally Reardon provided resource material, as did Peter Herrndorf. The staff at CTV's W5 patiently helped me find and screen decade-old tapes to assist my research. My editor, Charis Wahl, gave creative direction. And my brother, David Frum, provided many useful tips. But it is to my parents, Barbara and Murray Frum, that I wish to express my deepest gratitude. Without their advice, encouragement, and loving support, nothing, including this book, would be as much fun to do. My thanks to all.

Linda Frum
January 1990

INTRODUCTION

Does anyone watching the nightly news fail to experience, if only for a moment, a twinge of envy for the reporters who get to be right *there* as world events unfold? When Imelda flees without her shoes, when a budget document is stolen from Michael Wilson's office, when the Berlin wall is torn down, the men and women of the media see it up close. They hit the pulse points of the universe, order room service, and tell the rest of us what happened.

It seems to be a life of adventure and intrigue — and according to the forty-nine television journalists whose anecdotes and observations appear in this book, so it can be. But it is also a life of trudging, wheedling, and unreliable plumbing. Every flash of footage that catches Syrian shelling of some Lebanese stronghold necessitates hours of waiting for a connection in the Athens airport. Every glimpse of Mikhail Gorbachev represents days spent in gloomy Moscow hotel rooms.

Millions of us get most of our information about the world from television. The people who decide what to cover and how to present it hold enormous and insufficiently recognized power over their audience. To a very great extent those television journalists determine what our perceptions will be. They form our reality. Because of their power, we ought to know more about them: how they do their jobs, how they view their jobs, and what they do off-screen that might affect what gets on screen. That's what this book is about.

As editor, I had the pleasure of interviewing all of Canada's leading television journalists. I was armed with a battery of questions: Which were the worst war zones? How do you push your way to the front of a scrum? What's a hack hotel really like? What do you eat when you travel with the mujahideen? Which world leaders are the most appealing?

Hundreds of hours' worth of tapes produced more than a thousand pages of transcript. The chapters were organized according to natural divisions of the news-gathering process: the choice of stories, the techniques used to get those stories, the outrageous characters encountered on the way, the special perks and perils that appertain to the story-gathering, and, in the end, what these stories tell us about the national and international scenes.

Brian Stewart came up with an evocative and deeply moving portrait of what it was like to cover Ethiopia and Sudan during the great famines. Linden MacIntyre, reliving his memories of the brutal Lebanese civil war, could not hold back the tears in his eyes. Ann Medina, feverishly explaining the details of a harrowing event in Beirut, jumped vigorously around my apartment, re-enacting the scene, until I finally got the picture.

Peter Mansbridge's discussion of journalistic ethics was so absorbing, he finally had to break away from my pleas of "just one more question, just one more question" by explaining, "Look, Linda, the news starts in three minutes and I do have to be there."

After speaking to so many journalists it became clear that the typical television reporter is not necessarily the ridiculously brave, sexually insatiable, hot-tempered foreign correspondent of Hollywood's imagination. Most reporters spoke of the need for patience, and a willingness to submit themselves to a career where success is based largely on serendipity. Ann Medina insists, "What you need is stamina, a cast-iron stomach, a bladder that can stand hours without going, and no physical modesty."

From these interviews too, I learned about the capacity of television and its inherent limits. All of Canada's leading television reporters agree that it would be foolish for viewers to rely on television as their sole source of information. They concede that television can easily become shallow and biased, and is susceptible to distortion. Still, television's main virtues — its immediacy and emotional force — must also be appreciated.

To fully understand why communism collapsed in Eastern Europe, for example, one needs an economic analysis of the futility of central planning and a history course on Eastern European nationalisms. But equally, to appreciate what it *felt like* when communism collapsed, few would substitute the most learned book or periodical for a television set. Anyone without three free weeks to travel through the region, a speaking knowledge of German, Czech, and Hungarian, and the good luck to arrive in each place just as the excitement began, would see less of the revolutions of 1989 than would the most slovenly couch potato.

Moreover, in 1989, television was not just a source of information on events, it played a critical role. The brutal East German government did not shoot down the hundreds of thousands of protesters who thronged the streets, demanding democracy in November 1989. It surrendered. There is no single explanation for this decision, but it is clear that one reason was the Honecker regime's fear of the consequences of murdering its citizens in front of Western television cameras.

Television's influence on Eastern Europe's determination

to free itself from communism should not be underestimated. Luscious West German television commercials and smuggled American videocassettes showed people a better life. The TV reports beamed in from neighbouring countries already engaged in the struggle for democracy inspired the East Germans to follow. And, during the weeks of turmoil, first in Poland, then in Hungary, and, finally, in East Germany, the people who risked their lives in the streets knew they were safer when they saw the cameras and the trenchcoats of the Western media.

Of course, television does not topple an "evil empire" every day. Most of the time it covers floods in Flin Flon, and mud slides in Moncton. But its ability to make distant, unrelated souls care about one another is always there. And for that alone, television deserves its primacy.

WHAT IS NEWS?

Television news competes not only with other sources of news information — newspapers, magazines, and radio — but also with everything else on TV. Every television reporter is acutely aware that if a report fails to delight, amuse, or titillate as much as, say, an episode of *Knot's Landing* . . . ZAP! . . . the viewer is gone with a click. Not only must a television correspondent evade flying bullets, invade impenetrable battle zones, and duck officious bureaucrats, he must also disarm the TV-channel changer.

No self-respecting newspeople want to admit that their production values have anything in common with those of Lorimar or Aaron Spelling, but in their hearts they understand that they must measure up to those commercial television standards or else . . . oblivion.

The millions of Canadians who watch the news on television every day demand immediacy. If they wanted the facts alone, they would read a newspaper. They watch television because they want emotional involvement, if not the actual splatter of blood and gore. Our appetite for vicarious suffering causes the steady decline of standards of good taste; the walls of censorship are regularly torn down. There are no longer debates about whether rotting corpses should be shown on the air, only about how far back the camera should be. Still, even the audience has its limits. Each journalist must learn how to walk that fine line of discretion.

Some of the most difficult choices in broadcasting are between individual privacy and the public's right to know . . . and, of course, the network's need for ratings. **Peter Mansbridge**, *news anchor for the* CBC, *is part of the team at* The National *making the daily judgement calls on the images that will — and won't — be presented to the home viewers.*

If we ever showed everything that we have access to, people would be really upset. A lot of awful stuff comes in every day that we weed out. When something is borderline, then a group decision is made about how to deal with it.

One subject of a lot of debate was a guy under investigation in Pennsylvania who called a news conference, read a long prepared statement, and then pulled a gun out from his jacket. He stuck it in his mouth, said, "This is what you've always wanted," and blew his head off. It was very gruesome. The guy had called a news conference to commit suicide.

The tape went around the world like a rocket. It was put on every feed. There were those who argued: "Look, it's news. It happened. The guy was a public figure in this town. We should show the clip." Others said: "Sure it happened, he was a public figure, *but only in that town*. Why do *we* care? We care about him only because he blew his head off, and we don't cover suicides on *The National*."

It was very interesting to watch how each network dealt with the problem. In the end, we explained that this bizarre event took place, but showed only a picture of the guy with a gun in his mouth. I don't think any network ran it in its entirety, though they all chose a different point at which to get out. You could hear the gun go off, but they'd freeze the picture.

The day the shuttle [Challenger] exploded we were on the air for six or eight hours and, obviously, we were showing the explosion over and over again. In a way, it was sort of an "acceptable" explosion because it happened far away and you couldn't see human parts. But I suppose with the shuttle, we would have shown everything, no matter what it looked like.

During the shuttle broadcast, one of the producers said into my earpiece: "We've got incredible tape of McAuliffe's parents from before the explosion right through to the end. Intro it for us." But I just knew I didn't want to do it. They kept yelling, "Intro! Intro! Intro!" in my ear, but I finally just went to something else. When the camera came off me, I got on to the phone and said, "Look, it's too much. I don't want to use it."

They didn't agree with me, but the fact is, I'm in the driver's seat. They can't run the clip unless I introduce it. So we didn't. Other stations did, and thought it was an extremely moving and graphic revelation of what had happened. But I felt it was too great an invasion of the family's privacy.

The Pan Am crash near Lockerbie, Scotland, was a much different case. After that explosion, there were bodies hanging out of trees . . . we had access to that film but we didn't use it, although some of the newsweeklies did.

Some very gripping scenes were also shot at Kennedy Airport — mothers, fathers, sisters, brothers, crying, weeping, falling to the ground when they learned the news of the crash.

People from Pan Am would go up to them and say: "Are

you waiting for somebody from Flight 103?" And if they said yes, the official would say, "Come with us," before the family member reached the reporters. And then you'd hear them screaming and crying. It did tell an incredible story of human suffering, but we felt it was too much for us to show. In Syracuse, they ran it all, and defended their decision because there were twenty or twenty-five students from Syracuse who were on the plane.

Perhaps the most controversial item in terms of audience response was a piece on the El Salvador war, broadcast in the early 1980s. Joe Schlesinger was down there for us. He had gone to a number of towns that had been first captured by the rebels and then recaptured by the government. When he filed his story, he called up and said, "You're going to find some of these pictures very difficult to watch, but I think they tell the story."

His profile was the classic story of a little town where the guerrillas move in, shoot up a few soldiers, and take the town. Three hours later, the government comes in with helicopter gunships, kills all the guerrillas, and retakes the town. But this one was a little different. To show how much back in control they were, the government troops cut off all the heads of the guerrillas, and stood for the cameras with them in their hands.

Normally you wouldn't even think to show this stuff on the air. But here was Joe telling a news story, using incredible, graphic pictures so that, no matter what else you remember about El Salvador, you'll never forget this. It was pretty awful to look at, but it gave you, for that instant, a realization of the extent of the horror.

There was debate — a lot of debate — over this. There

were those who felt we absolutely couldn't run this. But Joe pleaded and pleaded his case, and it started to swing after a certain point. I mean, we didn't sit there, watching it over and over again; you only had to see it once. In the end, we decided to run it. We got a lot of mail. I think we got more mail on that than on anything we've ever run. People just couldn't believe we'd show it.

On the twenty-fifth anniversary of the big Air Canada crash outside Montreal, somebody on the local Montreal show found out that one of the policemen, who was there the night of the crash and tried to rescue people, went back every year to put flowers on the site. It was very touching, so off they went to film him doing it this year, the twenty-fifth year. They did an interview with him and got a clip of him saying that he remembered that, when he got there, there were heads all over the ground.

Shortly after, the Montreal station got a letter from a Calgary lawyer whose father had been on the plane and had died on the flight. He really thought it was disgusting that the CBC would run a clip like that. Why did he need to be reminded twenty-five years later of the possibility that his father had been decapitated?

They got the letter, and what do you say? They wrote back to say they were sorry and that they hadn't thought it through. I think they said they were sorry because, twenty-five years later, those who were directly affected by the crash do have a say in what the media does. When you have time to consider the implications, as we certainly did in this case, twenty-five years later, you must think about how the story will affect people.

I'm inclined to get very defensive very fast. It's probably one of my weaknesses. I immediately say we didn't do any-thing wrong. But there is no carved-in-stone rule of where you draw the line. You don't say: "We'll never show a severed head." Sometimes you need to do it to explain a story. In this business you can't go to a computer at the end of the day and say: "Okay here are all the decisions I made; tell me which ones were right, and which were wrong." It depends on the story, the day, the issue.

*CTV field producer **Malcolm Fox** is reluctant to shelter his audience from grisly scenes. He places realism — even graphic realism — ahead of squeamish sensibilities.*

We spent a week at the site of the Italian earthquake in 1976 so we could follow the process of digging through the rubble and finding victims. Of the scenes we saw there, the one I remember the most vividly is of an unearthed father, dressed in his underwear, lying on a couch with his year-old daughter in his arms. Their house had fallen down on top of them. We rolled film while people were uncovering them.

In those days, the decision of what the audience would see was made in Toronto and not in the field. We would send back the film, the script, the on-camera portions, and it would be assembled in Toronto. Today, the decison of what to show is made in the field. I always err on the liberal side. I believe we should be a window on the world. If it happened, we should show it. If the story is, this father tried to save his daughter and the house fell down on top of them, well then, however gory these pictures may be, they should be shown. It is possible to cut the pictures in such a way that they illustrate without dwelling on the gore.

Sometimes journalists push tenaciously to record footage they later find too upsetting to broadcast. Journal *reporter* **Linden MacIntyre** *resists showing his audience material so gruesome that it distracts from the message he wants to convey.*

We had to fight very hard to get past the guards at Sabra and Shatila after the massacre of Palestinians by Falangists there. We experienced a brief moment of triumph and then we smelled our surroundings. Rescue workers hovered around the scene, wearing surgical masks. As you came in, they handed you one.

I watched them hauling bodies out of the rubble. One woman's body was trapped under a load of debris in a house that had been dynamited. They would get her body out a little bit but then would have to move something else to get her out any farther. They used a front-end loader with a bucket to gingerly pick away the debris. I was standing right by the bucket when it crashed down and emptied its contents. Something went "splat" by my foot. There on the ground was the arm and little hand of a baby. It was the woman's child — what was left of it, anyway.

The rescue worker tenderly picked up the little arm and

put it on a stretcher, and I was standing there thinking: What do I do? Do I vomit? What do I do? I took refuge in my job and told the cameraman to shoot it. I wouldn't use the footage on air, but I felt it had to be shot. What else could I do? My role there was to document what was happening, no matter how ghastly. If I were wearing a Red Crescent, my role would be to dig out the bodies. If I was wearing a uniform, my job would be to maintain order. What does a reporter do? He records.

Reporter **Ann Medina** *insists that reporters' power to select what their viewers will see does not tempt them to deviate from strict objectivity.*

I see myself as a judge summing up the facts for the jury. I'm presenting the strongest case of each legitimate side. You may have feelings and you can't take them out of you, but you can fight them. You have to put them aside as much as possible. Some say there's no such thing as objectivity, so we wallow in subjectivity. That's baloney. Of course, there's no such thing as objectivity, but there are instincts inside all of us that recognize the difference beween being more and less objective. The big thing is, when you get close to a situation, you see the complexities. You see the greys.

While you're in Canada, you may have views about who's right and who's wrong, but when you arrive at the conflict spot, you soon realize how much more complex everything is. It's easier than people imagine to step back and give, if not a purely objective report, one close to it.

Objective or not, television news, according to CBC *European correspondent* **Patrick Brown** *is by definition limiting and distorting.*

One thing about broadcast journalism is that it is sequential. Because it's sequential, there's an implicit order of importance. Theoretically, the first story you are told is the most important, and the last one — the one you remember — is the least important. *The Times* of London used to print the Classifieds on the front page, leaving it to readers to find whatever interested them on the inside, not offering an implicit scale of values the way broadcast journalism does.

Access plays a large role in what gets covered. Until recently, nothing happened in Hungary because nobody was there. East Timor? It doesn't exist. The Burmese war has never gotten covered. There is so much going on in the world, you cannot know everything.

With national reporting you have to lay options and facts before people who are going to decide something for themselves. In foreign corresponding you are interpreting something that is going on in a distant place and making it understandable to Canadian people. For example, we're not trying to make Canadian people believe that Likud is better than Labour. What we are trying to do is reflect what the Israelis are thinking and doing. Consequently, it becomes very impressionistic.

During the riots in Yugoslavia during the winter of 1989, I was called upon to make judgements about why the Yugoslavs were doing what they were doing. Of course, these judgements have to be generalizations — I have two minutes of airtime. I have to say: "Yugloslavs have always been very concerned about . . ."

I don't get that information by doing a public-opinion poll. I do it by asking people what the problems are. It's not scientific. It's interpretive in a way that would get us fired instantly if we did it in Canada, and quite rightly.

Somebody once said that writing news is like Swiss cheese — you are writing around the holes. You just don't know some things. A novel is Cheddar cheese — all the necessary details are there. But journalism *is* writing around the holes. So, you write in such a way that you are not telling lies, but you are giving impressions. It's very pointillist, impressionistic.

Doug Small, *Ottawa bureau chief for* Global News, *explains one of the causes of the impressionistic quality of television: good pictures are easy to come by, even when a good story is not.*

You have to feed the goat. If you have an hour-long newscast, it has to be full. Sure, there are days when you have to struggle for a story, but you do it. In television, even if there's nothing to say, there's usually lovely pictures to say it with. You're never at a loss. The nervous tummy usually comes from the logistics of the thing — the difficulty of getting to a feed-point or being in a place that's got so much humidity, your gear goes down on you. Usually that's where your trouble comes from. It doesn't come from worrying about having something to say.

For example, on a leader's trip, the nice thing is that, if all else fails, there's always the itinerary. If a leader made a speech or visited a commune or saw a kibbutz, or whatever, you've always got an event that you can tie something on. Obviously there are times when the material is much better than at other times, and you want it to be as good as possible so that you'll appear as high up in the program as you can, but I can't remember a trip I've been on where there was, literally, nothing to file. If you're going to Senegal and there's no real news, you can always do a quick feature on a leper colony. The fact that leprosy still exists is interesting.

Identifying and broadcasting the real news from inside the democratic world is hard enough. Former BBC *correspondent* **John Bierman** *explains why trying to do it from a repressive Islamic nation is especially taxing.*

I always say any damn fool could get thrown out of Iran by Khomeini. It took a bit of class to get thrown out by the Shah. I opened the BBC bureau in Teheran in 1972 and was thrown out in 1973. The Shah's Iran was a pretty thoroughgoing police state. He was an absolute monarch, his power was all pervasive. His secret police, SAVAK, were into everything. There were spies everywhere.

The local media was totally censored; no bad news was ever published. It was very difficult to find out what was happening in the country because people were too afraid to talk. We reported on the student unrest, the executions without trial, the human-rights violations. I'm told the Shah would listen to the BBC every morning, and, if he couldn't listen, he'd have the transcripts brought to him to read in bed.

The Brits were selling the Shah an enormous number of Chieftain tanks, at that time the most advanced battle tanks in the world. Since the Brits were making vast amounts of money out of tank sales to Iran, the Shah thought that all he had to do was to tell the British ambassador to tell the British Government to tell me to shut up. When the ambassador told him, "I'm sorry, Your Majesty, but we don't have any control over what the BBC says or does," the Shah saw this as a terrible weakness and one of the reasons why Britain was going downhill.

One of the BBC current-affairs shows, *Panorama*, decided to do a half-hour piece on the Shah. I had absolutely nothing to do with it. When the Shah read the *Panorama* transcript, he was so incensed he told his people to throw me out. They told him: "We can't throw him out, Your Majesty, he's not here." The Shah said: "Well, as soon as he's back, throw him out!"

Political coverage of Ottawa has changed drastically since 1977, when the House of Commons first allowed television cameras into the chamber. Now, rather than having to rely on second-hand summaries of what was said, footage of the indignation, fierce determination, and stormy patriotism of our politicians is available to us each night. Of course, all that emotion would be a lot easier to take if we didn't have this gnawing feeling that it was put on for the cameras. CTV *Ottawa correspondent* **Alan Fryer** *explains why we're right to worry.*

The strength of TV is pictures, and one of the problems of being a TV reporter in Ottawa is that the stories we cover aren't visual. Ottawa is the continuing story of man or woman walking into room, walking out of room, walking down steps, walking up steps, sitting around the table looking stupid. That's what we have to work with. So, to punch up our pieces, we have to use the theatre of Question Period. And, to be honest about it, even if the theatre doesn't exactly relate to a piece, we'll try to accommodate it. We need something to spice up our piece, otherwise we'll have a nation of people clicking their TV remotes, asking: "Martha, is there anything else on tonight?"

That's where the politicians manipulate us. They know exactly what we're looking for. We need short and punchy. So, if Mr. Turner stands up and starts pounding his desk, shouting: "Mr. Speaker, there's a cover-up going on!" — well, it may be bullshit, but he knows we're going to use it. If the opposition's first question doesn't get a good answer, they use their supplementary question to slip in the theatrics: "When are you going to come clean with the Canadian people?" Accusations work. That's why you'll often see the same clip on all networks. We're all looking for the same thing.

During Question Period, CTV's *weekly look at politics on the Hill,* **Pamela Wallin,** *staked some new territory when she asked a politican point-blank about whether he had a drinking problem. The question aroused the disapproval of colleagues and the wrath of her audience. Apparently, there are still some frontiers of decorum many Canadians do not want a reporter to cross, even if not crossing them deprives viewers of information we may have a right to have.*

When I asked John Turner if he had a drinking problem, it was not something I did lightly. I mean, you just don't raise that kind of problem on national TV without thinking seriously about it.

We were heading into an election year and this man wanted to be prime minister. Too many people — in his caucus, on the Hill, in the press corps — had witnessed it too many times. Too many people were pointing the finger.

There are lots of things people do in their "personal" lives that you or I may find objectionable. But if it doesn't influence their work, it's none of our business. If a cabinet minister wants to have unconventional relationships, well, as long as that doesn't influence his ability to carry out his duties, it doesn't matter. But if his ability is affected, then the matter becomes a public question.

I thought Turner handled the question very well. But I got a lot of heat for asking it. My feeling was that it was better to do it on our show than in a scrum. If you are going to raise that kind of an issue, you have to give the person a reasonable amount of time to respond. You can't do it at the three o'clock scrum, with a mike shoved in their mouth, between questions on free trade.

Yes, we do invade people's lives. But people who run for public office forfeit their right to complain about that. They sign a blank cheque when they embark on public life. Even those of us on television have figured that out. We are public property, too, and people can say what they want about us.

Whatever a reporter's views on the right to privacy of public figures, CBC science and medical reporter **Eve Savory** *tries to protect the dignity of her less well-known subjects, even as she exposes their suffering.*

For a piece on euthanasia, I interviewed a woman who had Lou Gehrig's disease, which paralyses your entire body. All she could move was her eyes. She was weeks from death. I asked her if she wanted the doctors to take "heroic measures" to end her life. Because she couldn't speak, all she could do was move her eyes back and forth to signal that, "yes" she did. I went away and I just felt like I wanted to throw up.

Her husband sat next to her, weeping. He was feeding her chocolates. She wasn't allowed to have them and they would melt on her lips. She couldn't swallow, and chocolate trickled down her neck. It was heartbreaking. As we filmed this, I had this sense of terrible invasion into someone's dying moments.

I found the physician who was in charge of palliative care, and I told her I was really traumatized by the interview. I didn't know if I should put it on the air. The doctor said, "You should know that Mrs. MacDonald wanted so much to do this. It was her way of leaving the world something and feeling like her death was not totally in vain."

It touched me so much that this woman wanted to leave something positive behind. Sure, I invade people's space at times. But I never do it without making it really clear what type of invasion it is going to be. I always talk with the cameraman to make sure these stories are done as sensitively as possible. The story of Mrs. MacDonald really mattered.

Once I understood that people let you into their lives for a reason, I felt better about what I do. What's more, if I can tell their story in such a way that they do not feel betrayed or raped, then I feel I've done something good.

In the war between press and politicians for control of the medium's message, **Andy Moir**, *an editor for the* CTV National News, *admits that politicians usually win. This is most evident during election campaigns when the parties' back-room boys set an agenda that the media obediently follow.*

On election campaigns, we are too tied to the damned leader. They have press planes, and we go on them. But, in the process of agreeing to follow the leader's tour, you are agreeing to be manipulated. Just the logistics require that you be manipulated in the most basic sense. They have to get everybody on and off the planes. They have to take us to the hotels, check our baggage. You know damned well that there are a lot of staged events you are expected to cover dutifully. They find colourful areas to take people to so that there is a nice backdrop. They're all very clever. They used to be concerned only about making the nightly *National News* at ten and CTV at eleven. So, they staged their major events in the evening, until they discovered that the audiences of the six o'clock newscasts are much more massive — almost double. Since 1984, they have begun staging afternoon events to get on the early-evening news service so they get twice the exposure.

It's a very expensive proposition, flying around with these people. You pay to be on the plane. You pay through the nose. It's first class plus fifty per cent, and it's not even a logical way to cover an election in the first place.

Still, in many ways our coverage of Ottawa is much more intelligent than it used to be. Watergate was the seminal event that made journalists realize that they have a role to play — to legitimately challenge. We will never go back to the bad old days when our idea of covering the Hill was to let John Diefenbaker talk as long as he wanted into our microphones unchallenged. When you look back at some of those old newscasts, it's embarrassing. They're like propaganda films.

Though the world is teeming with tragedies and travesties, only nine or ten reach viewers of The National *each night. Television journalists must decide which stories deserve the precious airtime. By their own admission, what wins out is not always the most important story, but the one with the greatest potential to entertain. Television journalists are under enormous competitive pressure to give people what they want. As* **Elly Alboim**, *the Ottawa bureau chief for the* CBC National News, *points out, what gets on air is journalists' assessment of the taste and appetite of the audience: we get the news we deserve.*

Television has very little to contribute to the readers of *The Financial Post, The Globe and Mail, Saturday Night*, or other sophisticated media sources. Without being too cynical about this, if we can slip in one or two items of significance a day, we feel we are holding back the Huns a bit.

The Canadian elite spends $25,000 a year for newsletters, which give them substantial information and the highest quality of journalism in the country. For the rest of the country, television has a social responsibility to make the information it provides less consumer driven and more substantive, in order to bring up the level of national discourse.

Whenever you do any analysis of the kind of information that consumers want, weather leads the list, followed by health, medicine, and science stories second, and personality news third. The desire for stories about the economy, politics, and labour is always at the bottom.

Still, whenever there's a dramatic international story, our audience size doubles. People want to see major events — large air crashes, civil wars, invasions — with their own eyes. They may not care about what our reporter has to say about what John Turner said today, but they want to see John Turner say it.

Unfortunately, any Canadian citizen whose world view is formed by listening to easy-listening radio, reading a tabloid in the morning, and watching one of the network newscasts at night does not have enough information to manipulate his environment and protect himself from outside forces.

The National is doing the best it can with twenty-two minutes. But twenty-two minutes is ultimately nine stories — print's news-hole is four hundred times the size of TV's. Compression forces us constantly to make a set of brutal choices. Which nine stories do you choose? There is no virtue in producing nine stories of real substance and detail and have them watched by only 150,000 people. How is that going to solve the problem? My concern is that the mass of the Canadian population is not getting suffcient information. Is the solution to provide a program they won't watch?

Some of the best journalistic minds in the country work in TV. There is no lack of intellectual ability among TV journalists, and the players on the Hill have as much respect for TV journalists as the print journalists.

Around here, I'm known as "Public Policy Alboim" because I believe our news priorities are wrong. We're in the flavour-of-the-month business. I could have done with fewer AIDS stories. I know it's a human tragedy, but there are a lot more issues that affect a lot more people. And after you've made a general statement about an issue, to continue to provide a roster of examples day after day dulls the educative function, and skews the news because other stories are being displaced.

During the National Agricultural Conference in 1985, our bureau did a piece for the news that included a clip from the prime minister, a clip from the agriculture minister, and charts about the price of barley, oats, and wheat. *The National* decided our story was too complex. Instead, they went to Manitoba to talk to Harry and Ethel on the farm. They pushed the buttons on their little calculator, looked into the camera, and said that the new agricultural program didn't work for them.

The common wisdom in Canadian journalism is that information is more relevant when it's personalized. So, if you can start off a piece with "Jane Doe is thirty-two years old, lives in Halifax with three kids, and doesn't like child care," journalists accept that, somehow, Jane makes day care more understandable. If you really believe you can tell anything, moving from the specific to the general, if you don't understand that the specifics box you in and give you only a small slice of the general, there is something wrong with you. Still, there is a cultural value in my organization and every other news organization in this country that says it is better journalism to talk to Harry and Ethel, or Jane.

I would like to reweight the news, concentrating on economic and political levers rather than the idiosyncratic, the slice-of-life, the personalized. People are not turning on the news to find themselves reflected in it. Do we have to do every interest-rate story as a function of some young couple in Toronto looking for a house and not being able to find one? Part of the inability to raise the level of national debate in this country stems from our desire to make Harry and Ethel feel comfortable with their level of understanding.

The need for visuals is the most overstated excuse for the lack of content on TV. Sure, the language of television is inherently visual. Nobody disputes that. There is a structure in television that demands conflict, denouement, and conclusion. Computer-generated graphics allow you to visualize virtually anything. But, still, it is hard for me to get some stories on the air. It's not that we can't visualize stories about the economy, for example. But in our consumer-driven model of journalism, we do not give our audience something for which they lack an appetite.

In an earlier era of journalism, reporters and the politicians
they covered treated one another as respected colleagues
rather than mortal enemies. **Knowlton Nash** *reflects on*
how these friendlier relations affected political coverage.

I covered John Kennedy when he was running for president.
In those days, you got to know people more readily than
today. The change has come mostly for security reasons, but
also because so many more people follow the political leaders
today. Then, there were about fifteen of us following Kennedy around during his efforts to win the Democratic
nomination.

One time, we were in some hotel, in some small town,
somewhere in the Midwest. Kennedy never carried any
money — ever. In the hotel lobby, he saw a magazine he
wanted to buy. Since he didn't have any money, he turned to
me and asked if I would lend him five dollars, adding: "I'll get
it back to you for sure." That's the last I ever saw of it. He was
always short of money, particularly on the road. Credit cards
were fairly new at that point but he didn't use those either.

I followed both Dukakis and Bush in the last campaign, and
the change from then till now is quite startling: you just never
get close. In Canada, too, you can't get as close as you used to
get with Pearson or Diefenbaker. One explanation is that
today nothing is off the record. Before, when you were
travelling with a political leader, a lot was off the record. You
just didn't report some things. But you accumulated the
knowledge about the human being you were following so you
were able to give a more rounded story about him later on.

Today we have less ability to understand the human being
behind the policies than we had before.

A hot story from a reliable source doesn't always guarantee a reporter top spot on the evening's line-up. Cautious executive producers, fussy lawyers, and other assorted big shots must approve. Because of this, CTV's **Robert Hurst** *will not be remembered as the man who broke the story of the Mulroney government's "tuna crisis" even though he was the first to get the tip, the first to track down the story, and the first to talk to the minister concerned. He had everything he needed to break the story — except the enthusiasm of his network.*

One night in May 1985, I got one of those classic calls that instructed me to go to a phone booth. Now, if a source calls me and asks me to go to a phone booth, I don't say "Don't be a jerk," I go.

It was very late at night and I was working in our Ottawa bureau. The man on the telephone tells me that there's a huge problem in the Ministry of Fisheries. I asked him what the problem was, and he says: "Stinky fish. They took hundreds and hundreds of cases of this stuff and tried it out on the military, and the soldiers got sick." He didn't have the whole story, but he said the ministry was approving rancid tuna for sale.

René Lévesque died suddenly that night so I had to drop the tuna story, but worked quietly on it through June. Some cooks at the Department of National Defence had said the tuna was junk and sent it back. They put it in quarantine and I shot some pictures of that. We took pictures of the Starkist plant and interviewed some workers.

On the Friday of the Canada Day weekend, I went to

interview John Fraser, the Minister of Fisheries, a wonderful, honest guy, who says right off: "I know all about it. It's a mess. Turn on your camera and I will tell you about it." And he did.

He explained that, when he came in as minister, the company appealed to him that they had this whole warehouse full of cans of rejected fish. And he said to me, on camera: "I decided to give the company the benefit of the doubt. I had it independently inspected in New Brunswick, and it was confirmed to me that there was no health hazard, no one was going to die, it was just sub-quality tuna fish. And I decided to give the company the benefit of the doubt." That's what he said.

So I have the story. And it's a fucking good story. First week of July — no one else has this story. But CTV is really worried. "Get those tuna inspection reports," say CTV and the lawyers, "and we'll go with the story."

Second week in July, Starkist brings action in the Federal Court of Canada to block release of the inspection records, as is their right. As soon as Starkist brought that action, the story became public: CTV is trying to get tuna inspection records.

I've got this wonderful story and my company won't go with it until they have the records. Starkist is stalling. And then, the *Fifth Estate* gets on to the story in the middle of August. I know that they're on to it because one of the guys in the Department of Fisheries calls me: "Did you know that Eric Malling was over here asking exactly the same questions that you were asking in June?" Thank you very much for reminding me.

I called my guys in Toronto and said the *Fifth Estate* is on to the story, let's go with it. They said: "No, we'll wait." It was a huge fight between CTV and me. There was blood on the floor.

In September, the *Fifth Estate* ran the story as the lead item of their season opener. They worked on the story for two weeks and broadcast an interview with the minister. They bought a can of Starkist, and Eric Malling opened it up and said: "Oh, that doesn't look very good to me." They had no pictures from inside the plant, no pictures of the tuna that had been quarantined, none of the tuna inspection reports. But the CBC didn't care about the inspection reports. They weren't as cautious as our libel lawyers were.

The CBC broke the story at nine, or whenever the *Fifth Estate* goes on. I wanted to put our story up that night as a matcher. But CTV said no. The next day, the scandal broke. I went out and got drunk for three days.

During the national debate on free trade, Canadians spent a lot of time contemplating the differences between us and the Americans. Of one distinction we can be sure: we don't spend the mega-bucks on news that they do. Every year, each American network spends roughly $200 million on news programming. The CBC, our biggest network, spends about a quarter that much. This dollar distinction reveals itself most acutely when Canadians compete head-on against the "Amnets" for international news. Do bigger bucks make for better news? Yes. **Brian Stewart** *insists that Canada's lack of international importance can sometimes liberate Canadian television, for it doesn't have the Amnets' need to tie their news to the foreign-policy objectives of their government.*

The American networks have a clear mindset: What does it mean for Washington? How will the president handle this? How will it affect our relations abroad? It is a kind of imperial outlook, easy to develop if you're a superpower. In a sense, it's easier to write for the Amnets because the focus is always so sharp. In international relations, if it doesn't affect the United States, it scarcely exists.

As a Canadian reporter, you're much more eager to paint the broad picture; you usually are not much concerned with Ottawa's reaction, as Canada is often only peripherally involved. You can go to town on the intricacies of power relationships — and your editors back home have a greater patience with the soft shadings of a story.

For example: covering Lebanon for the Canadians you can

delve at some length into interfactional rivalries and cultural differences; the Amnets will fret about whether U.S. forces will be dragged in, or how Israel will cope. And when I went into southern Sudan for NBC, and came back with clear evidence that a massive famine was starting, NBC stuck it on a shelf for two weeks before slipping it on as a closing item on a weak-news night. It wasn't part of their focus. The CBC would have led with it.

The Amnets are interesting places to work, in that they resemble courts of the Italian Renaissance — plots, factions, favourites, intrigue, and threats. Marvellous theatre! Before going to NBC, I assumed those at the heights of network news were motivated by normal greed and ambition. I discovered the real propulsion was fear. Producers and reporters live in holy terror of even minor failures. Any setback is career threatening . . . and, so, one naturally pours a maximum amount of money into any venture: more crews, more cars, more chartered flights, more interpreters — the safest thing is to outspend all opposition. The thought of the competitors winning a story is so awesome that I've seen mature Amnet producers reduced to a state of panic, unable to function.

Canadian news is usually quite the opposite. On foreign stories, one isn't terribly concerned about what your Canadian opponent is doing. Sometimes I feel we aren't competitive enough. But we march to our drum and they march to theirs, which sometimes makes for quite good journalism. I found that an Amnet editor in New York can tell you in minute detail every aspect of the coverage done by your competitor. CBC editors rarely had a clue what CTV had done. They were interested mainly in meeting our "mandate." The

CBC was to do its thing regardless, which is a pleasant regime to work for most of the time.

I was surprised, when I first went to NBC, by the number of perks that were showered down on me, the humble reporter. Later, I grew suspicious of them, and in time even began to dislike them intensely. I remember going to Stockholm on a breaking story to find four massive limos waiting for our chartered executive jet. I had one, the producer another, the crew a third, and our "unit manager," who was there to pay the bills, had the fourth. It was embarrassing . . . we rode through the streets like a royal procession. The police were tempted to salute.

On assignment, I found myself surrounded by researchers and office staff eager to get me food or drinks, producers who wanted to do all the leg-work, and crews who sat around entirely at my disposal. It was like skating through cotton candy, and I felt farther and farther away from the story itself.

In the field, it was a grind with them as well. Their crews are excellent. But there was always much more of a rush; always an expensive rented plane waiting to sweep one back to a feed-point.

I used to be astonished by the amount of money thrown around, but I was also there long enough to see the end of the Golden Age of the Amnets. By 1986, austerity hit them as well. First CBS, then NBC, began a savage belt-tightening. I, an old veteran of CBC austerity, nodded sagely as I saw all the signs of an economic plague creeping into our lives. First, as always, our newspapers were cut back. Then office supplies started running short. In Frankfurt, our two drivers were reduced to one; then the one went part-time. Our security guard was fired, then promptly rehired in the panic following a Mid-East terrorist incident, then fired again in the sober light of dawn. Travel was cut back, and, when we went anywhere, it was with one crew instead of two. The lean years had arrived and one knew that the nearly mythical era of the networks' grandeur, the stories of rented 747s and limos beyond number, was fading into legend.

I should note, however, that I have a lot of time for Amnet reporters. The better ones are highly experienced and as good as you'll find anywhere. They work under far greater pressure and in the face of more daunting frustrations than their Canadian and British counterparts, and their end-product is often surprisingly good. Personally, I've found them to be intelligent, quick, courageous, and diligent. They have a higher sense of "quality control" in terms of facts than, say, the CBC normally has. They're extremely careful with facts and double-check sources relentlessly. They don't often make mistakes that can be avoided. And their investigative reporters simply have no equal that I know of.

Canadian journalism has some very real strengths. It tends, by and large, to be pretty fair-minded. But we also have some significant weaknesses. The terms "intellectually lazy" and "dull" often come to mind. God, we can be dull!

I'm not much of a true believer when it comes to journalism. I think we're pretty good town criers, but lousy prognosticators. Kay Graham of the *Washington Post* once said that journalism is the "rough draft of history." I couldn't disagree more. I spend a lot of time in print and television news archives and I'm always struck by how utterly wrong most news predictions turn out to be.

When I moved from print into television, around 1974, all us "Young Turks" sneered at the habit of so many older reporters to conclude each report with: "Only time will tell." Some of our impatience was justified — it was often simply a cop-out — but, in time, I think we replaced it with a rather arrogant and dubious claim to authority. We began to lecture on the likely course of future events; and tough no-nonsense predictions were demanded of reporters in the field. Most, knowing that our words would be likely forgotten a half-year hence, were happy to charge out on a limb. I think honest reporters will admit, in retrospect, that we were lucky to bat two hundred. Check the news archives of any period and you'll find them a strikingly inaccurate guide to future events.

I also think television in North America has a problem of underestimating the mental processes of our audience. It's there in the way we so desperately "focus" our stories. We have to have a "simple line," a firm "point of view," a clear sense of "conclusion." We hate it if an issue has too many complexities or if our politicians go on about "various options." But the world is far more complex than we suggest, and the affairs of nations incomparably more difficult to arrange. I think the British are far better at giving their audiences a sense of the range of options that exist on most issues. They're at their very best when they unravel complicated subjects; they show viewers the wide range of possibilities that are there for leaders to grapple with. They expect their audience to be able to keep up, and, of course, it can very well. Many outsiders often accuse journalists of being addicted to the simplistic. It's not a charge that is easy for us to duck.

Within our limits we can do a pretty good job, however, of portraying the cares and concerns of people. Competition has made our antennae very acute. And we are good fire-chasers. Modest-enough claims, perhaps, for a profession that could be more modest. But there you are . . .

Mark Phillips *has worked for both a Canadian and a U.S. network. He couldn't help noticing what money can buy.*

The Americans attack stories with sufficient resources to handle them. When I was overseas for the CBC, it was pretty dreadful. You would show up at a Northern Irish hunger-strike, which would drag on for weeks and weeks and weeks. You had one crew, maybe an editor, but probably not. The Americans would be there with six crews, five producers, and enough drivers to transport a small army. And yet, whatever we did was measured against what they did.

There are some advantages, though, in working for a network that doesn't have a lot of money to throw at things: you don't have to have a presence everywhere all the time. You are more selective in what you cover. The CBC can pick and choose where it wants to go. Besides, when you've been in Beirut for six weeks, it is sometimes a relief to know you have to go home because they've run out of money.

I covered the tanker war in the Gulf for CBS. The only way to cover that war was to fly around in helicopters at $2,000 an hour. We were running up absolutely spectacular bills. You'd go up there and fly through the mist of a hot August afternoon for six or eight hours, and you'd spent $20,000 for the day and see nothing but a little smoke.

Other networks attacked the war with varying sizes of bank accounts. NBC had a couple of helicopters plus a Twin Otter fixed-wing aircraft, spending amounts I couldn't even begin to calculate. The day the Americans hit one of the Iranian oil platforms, the only way to get the picture was with the Canadian-made Twin Otter. So, NBC had the only pictures of this burning platform. Is that worth a half a million bucks over a couple of months? I don't know.

The wedding of Prince Charles and Lady Diana Spencer was the world's most-watched broadcast: conservative estimates have it that five hundred million viewers tuned in, about one-tenth of the world's population. A couple of those millions were Canadians. **Barbara Frum**, *host of* The Journal, *went to London to comment on the glory and the grandeur of this great regal event for the penny-pinched* CBC. *Too bad she couldn't see a thing.*

There are many letdowns in broadcasting. When I was asked if I wanted to cover Charles and Diana's wedding, I said: "Sure! How glamorous! " Barbara Walters was there with her own Rolls-Royce. Peter Jennings was there with his own Rolls-Royce. The Americans had spread so much money over London, they could go wherever they wanted. No one was allowed to put a foot on the steps of St. Paul's. They could. ABC rented a bridge over the parade route with a perfect view of the church, and parked some anchor people there. Meanwhile, ten of us from CBC would pour out of a mini-Volkswagen. We were "covering" the wedding by following the BBC pool-feed on a monitor in the basement of a building in White City, fifty miles from London. We were nowhere near the parade route. We couldn't afford it.

During one slow moment, I announced that the Queen Mother's dress was sea green. And on my lousy monitor, it was. Back home, I received dozens of letters from people, mostly women, whose sets were far superior and said that, in fact, it was peacock blue. What could I do? We, who were supposed to have something brilliant to add to the event, were just watching the same television-feed as everybody else at home.

During the memorial service for those lost on the shuttle Challenger in the spring of 1986, Newsworld's **Alison Smith** *was flown down to Texas to cover this emotional event, which was to be broadcast live by the* CBC. *She couldn't see a thing either.*

After the Challenger blew up, I went down to Johnson Space Center in Houston to do a reaction piece from the memorial service. Actually, I wasn't at the service itself, but in a hangar half a mile away, watching on a monitor. Because my monitor was plugged into only one camera, I didn't see the cuts to President Reagan walking down a row of family members, hugging them as they cried.

Mansbridge and everybody in the control room in Toronto

were practically in tears watching this. Then they cut to me. I was as cool as a cucumber. I made my comments about Reagan's speech, but my tone obviously did not convey any of the overwhelming emotion people saw on their television screens. The producers in Toronto were baffled. It wasn't until I got home that I saw the footage I had missed.

Having worked for the CBC *as a correspondent in both Canada and the United States,* **Terry Milewski** *is impressed by the greater openness of U.S. society. For Canadian reporters, however, the chatty man in the street is unfortunately offset by the tendency of American bigwigs to give short shrift to reporters from the Great White North.*

Americans are so much more willing to talk to a camera than Canadians. I was in Miami, covering the race riots caused by tension between the black minority and the new Hispanic majority. The black community resents the flood of Hispanic refugees coming in, who seem to be getting a better deal out of America.

We were able to go anywhere we wanted. We got instant and unquestioning co-operation from city hall and from officials generally. We followed refugees getting their AIDS tests, being interviewed by social workers, giving their names, explaining their reasons for coming, and having their cases processed without anyone questioning our right to be there. The refugees were only too happy to tell their stories, and officialdom was glad to show that they were trying to help these people.

I can't imagine doing such a story and having access to such footage in Canada without eight months of preparatory suck-ing up to officials. It would be inconceivable. The usual questions — "Do you have permission to do this?" "Aren't you invading somebody's privacy?" "Isn't this too personal?" — never got asked. My explanation — America is a more open society.

If you want to do man-on-the-street interviews, which are not the most elevated form of journalism, but nevertheless can be revealing, you are much better off trying to do them in the States. On the day of the inauguration of President Bush, I stopped forty people to get a reaction, and only one person turned me down. The others just said: "Here's who I am and what I think."

In Canada, you'd get a much higher percentage of people who are cautious, wary, concerned about their image, worried about what their boss will think. They say to themselves: "Do I have permission to do this? Have I filled out the right forms?" It's a most striking difference between the two countries.

On the other side, America's political establishment is much more adept at controlling and manipulating television, and does it with a ruthlessness and relentlessness that we would not stand for in Canada.

Mulroney got hell for his cocoon strategy at the beginning of the '88 campaign. I'm told by one of his pollsters that he just couldn't get away with it. By contrast, George Bush did get away with it. I don't remember any sustained drumbeat of complaints from the media. They are very deferential.

I think American reporters are overly respectful. The White House press corps are highly paid people who are keenly aware of the intense competition for their jobs. They value their access so highly that they become like police reporters who, in order to get access to the local hostage incident, agree not to mention abuses in the police department.

I think the problem of journalism anywhere, and Canadians are not exempt, is that access becomes so precious, you have to be very nice to the people who mete it out. I see it on TV every night. Everybody always said: "Wasn't Sam Donaldson of ABC hard on Reagan?" I didn't notice that. I noticed him asking questions in a very loud voice. He got his questions answered, and he perhaps got farther than many others did. But I didn't notice him following up some of the disasters of the Reagan presidency, which made Reagan a laughingstock overseas but not among the White House press corps.

Of course, the access I have in Washington as a foreign reporter is bottom of the barrel. You have to worm your way in between CNN and the *Tallahassee Gazette*. There is a story told about a Canadian reporter from *La Presse*. His press card was mistyped by a secretary to read: "L.A. Press." Suddenly, he found all doors open to him. Correctly typed, and they would have said: "*La Presse*? What's that? Foreign?"

I find it difficult getting calls returned: "What's that? CBC? Did you say CBS? Oh, CBC. Is that the Centre for Disease Control?" The Canadian press corps tends to huddle together and share sad stories. We like to joke about the editors in Toronto who call to ask why we haven't got some major cabinet secretary to talk. We have to explain a hundred times that Senator Whatsit doesn't have any votes to lose in Toronto.

What's changed lately is that the CBC has actually been able to teach the shrinking American fat cats a few things about doing it on the cheap. They used to look down on us as these poor boys who had to sit at the back of the bus rather than chartering a Lear jet. Now that they are cutting costs, too, and are also sitting on the back of the bus, they look at us with new respect.

GET THE STORY!

Television is a cumbersome, logistically demanding medium. Bringing pictures of the Gorbie-and-Georgie love-in to your screen requires the services of a cameraman, a soundman, a field producer, an on-air reporter, and two vans to carry the tons of equipment. Then, after flying around the globe, endlessly loading and off-loading heavy, awkward cases of gear (a customs officer's delight, a punchy reporter's nightmare), the journalist must sweet-talk his way into places he's not welcome.

Television news needs the co-operation of its subjects and, understandably, they're often reluctant. Grief-stricken victims, foreign big shots uncertain of Canada's location on the map have good, sometimes overwhelming reasons not to talk to the reporters scurrying after them.

And yet, night after night, news programs are filled with polished, sophisticated, seemingly effort-free reports. How do they do it?

Reporters are not entirely forthcoming. They don't reveal how they manage to know so much about Uzbekistan on twenty-four hours' notice. Nor do they tell all the secrets of how they beat the competition. Paradoxically, however, TV reporters are proud of how they share in order to keep the news coming. Compared to print journalism, television journalism is a surprisingly co-operative, in some instances even collusionary enterprise. CBC shares material with NBC, CNN, and CBS, while CTV has access to material from CBS, NBC and ABC.

Without these agreements, which allow for the exchange of footage, facilities, reports, and information,

Canadian networks would be overwhelmed by the task of bringing their viewers the world.

Even between rival Canadian networks, there is the occasional sharing of tape. "If a colleague from another network screws up a shot, we will, informally and unofficially, pass along a copy of our tape," cameramen will tell you. "The next time it could be you who needs the favour."

At the crack of an assassin's gun, the rev of a tank engine, or the announcement of an arms treaty, disciplined foreign correspondents hurl themselves on to the first available airplane. They consider the consequences of what they're doing only once the in-flight service has begun. Reporters usually leave home with little psychological preparation for the task that awaits them. There's just no time. But as CBC's **Brian Stewart** *explains, such frenetic activity eventually exacts its toll.*

A news crew has an experience quite different from that of aid workers or military units in that there's rarely an acclimatization period — time to ease oneself physically and emotionally into trouble spots. The military believes it takes up to *three weeks* to adequately acclimatize units to hotter weather in crisis zones. Tension, heat, and dehydration are a dangerous mixture and have to be watched carefully. We usually race directly from air-conditioned hotel to crisis zone. You get up from your crisp sheets in the hotel, have a last cooling shower, and take off into the field for a week or two. This isn't a good way to operate — but we have no option.

A reporter, producer, cameraman, and sound technician have to lug about twenty pieces of luggage into the countryside . . . tripods, cassettes, batteries, spares for everything, food, medicine, sleeping bags, mosquito nets, bullet-proof vests (when necessary) clothes, and God knows what else. There's usually a guide-interpreter along as well, so, cramming ourselves and all our gear on to available charter flights and mini-vans is always a struggle.

It's all rather like a safari in which every hour contains a nasty surprise: a scheduled relief-flight never arrives, a van breaks down, the local police chief refuses to recognize our travel permits, the guide gets us lost, a delegation of Mother Teresa's nuns suddenly occupies the rooms we were promised in the only rest centre (and just try evicting them!). On and on it goes, crises large and small. With experience, one learns to take it all in stride and to try to get out of it what humour one can.

A typical day in the field usually starts around 5:00 a.m. when I wake up sweat-sodden on a crumpled cot after a restless sleep. The sheets and I are sticky from insect lotion. I wonder where the hell I am, then notice the thatched roof, dirty floors, the line of insects on the ceiling, and remember with a groan. The day ahead wil be another scorcher, and we'll be spending hours in spine-jarring travel to and from refugee camps. Somewhere along the way, I'll have to compose, write, and perform some on-cameras, which, weeks later, will somehow have to fit the story. If this is a documentary shoot, I'll have, at least, a decent amount of time. If news, we'll be racing frantically all day to get our pictures shot and on a plane back to a distant feed-point.

Drivers assume an incredible importance in our lives. They race your tape to the airport at breakneck speed and help you hurry it through customs. They are often the factor that decides whether a trip is a wild success or a humbling disaster. The good ones are invaluable, and a reporter will hoard his small collection of decent drivers like gold. Any treachery is justified to keep them out of the hands of the opposition. The worst curse you can ever wish upon a competitor is a lousy driver; the best ones are superstars within the business, relentlessly pursued by offers of work.

In Beirut, ABC had a chief driver whose fame within the business was far greater than that of the reporters he worked for. A calm teetotaller who inspired total confidence in his charges.

The best drivers are usually working for the Amnets by the time we arrive, but we've had some good ones . . . and a few who were terrible. I had one who was so stoned on hash every day that each trip became a to-hell-and-back adventure. Once, in the northern Lebanese port city of Tripoli, we were covering the fierce fighting around the harbour as the PLO were being driven into yet another exile. The city was a rubble-strewn killing ground, with particularly deadly gunmen who specialized in neat head-shots. I needed to do a stand-up in a location at least calm enough that my knees would stop shaking for a few minutes. I asked the driver to head for a quiet spot . . . we immediately bolted forward, zigzagging like maniacs through the rubble. On one right turn, I was horrified to see we were driving right into the contested port where two thousand fighters were in a last-ditch stand within the most dangerous square mile on earth.

"Mustafa," I bellowed, as I ducked for the floor, "I said take us to a *quiet* spot."

"Quiet?" He laughed. "I thought you said take me to the snipers! Here's where most of them are . . ."

On another occasion, this time in the Shuf Mountains where Christians and Druze were in a fierce war, he pulled the car over to the side of a road, missing by inches a still-unexploded mortar shell, which stuck absurdly out of the sand. Staring at the shell, we froze in horror as he picked up a huge rock and slammed it down right beside the shell. "This will warn others from hitting it," he said, as we dove for the ditch.

In most of the world, you can expect to be buffeted by bureaucracies. The army usually hates the ruling party, the party officials loathe the relief officers, the foreign ministry is detested by everyone, the regions hate the capital, the capital ignores the regions. And so it goes.

The biggest problems are hassles from local authorities. Long, tedious hours are spent arguing, very politely, that one has a right and a duty to take pictures in the area. One struggles with a blizzard of details, passes, visas, letters of introduction, telexes, internal forms, etc., etc.; one invariably gets caught up in quite fathomless bureaucratic wars. And often, the very people you want to help or whose plight you want to bring attention to, are the most trying to deal with.

In Ethiopia, local party cadres detest the government relief organizations and vice versa. So, your media pass from one can lead to contemptuous dismissal by the other. In southern Sudan, the relief organization is similarly reviled by southern soldiers. I've flown in with the personal blessing of the relief director, only to be immediately booted out by the troops.

As a rule, the lower down one goes in a bureaucracy, the more arrogant the officials. Left-wing local police tend to be stubborn obstructionists; right-wing locals are simply terrifying. But armed irregulars are the most dangerous breathing objects on earth, and the younger they are, the more dangerous. Lebanese roadblocks, manned by semi-literate teenage thugs, are an obvious case in point. But nothing chills my blood like a carload of armed civilians in Central America that seems persistently curious about my movements.

The CBC's **Eve Savory** *explains the trauma of getting to the satellite-feed on time.*

In June 1988, I went to Stockholm to cover the fourth International Conference on AIDS. Three of us — with twenty-one pieces of luggage . . . a suitcase each and eighteen cases — BIG, heavy cases of — gear.

The flight left Toronto at 4:00 p.m. Saturday and arrived in Stockholm, after two stopovers, around 5:00 p.m. Sunday. This kind of schedule makes me crabby. I was to get crabbier. Sweden's egalitarian society appears not to allow for porters. Three exhausted, crabby people manhandled seven luggage carts loaded with huge cases miles through the airport and customs into the rental car.

Crabby became downright bitchy two hours later when we saw our rooms in our wee hotel tucked away in the old town. They were about five by seven — one could barely turn around, let alone store our massive cases. So, we lugged them down steep stone stairs to the cellar — and every morning we had to lug them up for the shoot.

Breakfast is included in Swedish hotels and the food is splendid. It was important to stoke up at breakfast and to fill purses and camera cases with rye bread and cheese because, by the time we'd finish our feed, around midnight, the city's restaurants would have been closed for two hours. Stockholm is a magnificent city but it has a sober soul and goes to bed early.

One night we decided to cover a memorial march for people with AIDS — at dusk. Dusk in June in Stockholm happens VERY LATE. The drill was this: a cab would take

Bobby Whyte, the cameraman, to town, drop him off with the marchers, and then take the stand-up gear (tripod, lighting kit, microphones) to the square where the march would end. In the meantime, I would lay down my voice track, leave the piece to be edited, and take another cab to meet Bobby and the gear at the square. There we would do the stand-up, with the marchers arriving in the background.

The reporter can spend hours writing wise words and carefully choosing the perfect background for a stand-up. All the viewer notices, however, is that the reporter is looking tired, or is wearing a new jacket, or has gained more weight or lost more hair.

All went beautifully — I arrived at the square just as the march appeared off in the distance . . . and, yes, there was Bobby, taking pictures of the marchers carrying their candles through the gathering dusk. But where was the cabdriver with the tripod, the microphone, the lights? Vanished . . . Anyone who saw that stand-up might have noticed it was a wee bit shaky — Bobby was hand-holding the camera. It was also hard to see my face — the only lighting was the candles held by the marchers. And the sound was, to be kind, ghastly — picked up by the little mike on top of the camera.

The cabdriver? His dispatcher traced him two hours later, having a long coffee. With the meter running. But, we made the feed . . .

"Making the feed" is what it's all about in TV. A quick and dirty piece of news that makes your deadline is far better than a thoughtful, organized piece that doesn't. Trouble is, we all want to do both — that is, make our deadline and make it perfect. There lies the danger.

The last night of the conference, the producer and I decided we had to have a stand-up in Stockholm, even though the conference — and the feed-point — were half an hour away, in a Stockholm suburb. Our last feed-time for that night was 9:30 p.m. I had written the script and run it by the editor in Toronto to make sure fatigue and hunger (six days of no supper) hadn't so muddled my brain that I had said something libellous, stupid, or incomprehensible. I had laid down a voice-track for the editor and producer to work with and taken off in a cab with Bobby to do the stand-up. Bobby, you must understand, is a brilliant cameraman: his sense of lighting and pictures is magic. And he won't settle for anything less than magic. He had an image of a scene with ancient buildings climbing to the sky, with the golden light hitting the water just so. . .

To the consternation of our cabdriver, we insisted on being driven around Stockholm to look for the perfect backdrop. Dusk was falling and the clock was ticking. Each time I saw something that looked good, Bobby would point out that the framing was wrong or the lighting wouldn't work, etc. By 8:40 I was getting very panicky and insisted that we pull off a "q and d" (quick and dirty) stand-up in the middle of a bridge. It had water and buildings. It would do. We finished at 9:00 p.m. Half an hour to make the half-hour drive, plug the stand-up onto the end of the piece, tear over to the feed-point, and line up bars and tones and all those other things that producers have to worry about.

Luckily our driver's limited English did include the phrase "go like hell" — and he did. Until we hit the drawbridge. It was up, so we sat there. And sat. As the clock ticked and ticked. After some minutes, the driver walked up to the front of the line and learned that the bridge was stuck open. There were other bridges, but we were boxed in.

I leaped out, grabbed the tape, crawled on my knees under two rows of fences, darted through four lanes of speeding traffic, ran half a kilometre, leaped into an empty cab, waved money in the driver's face, and begged him to get me to the conference centre OVER ANY OTHER BRIDGE PLEASE, AND IN TEN MINUTES. Bobby and I spent one hundred dollars on cabs that night. I aged three years. But yes, we made the feed.

And the stand-up? Yes, the building reflected in the water behind me, and the golden lighting was perfect. But no one noticed, of course. The only comment was from my mother: was that a new jacket I was wearing?

The Journal's **Bill Cameron** *on the not-so-glamorous life of foreign correspondents:*

The truth is that life on the road is mostly schlepping. Hours, many hours of schlepping heavy steel cases of camera gear on to luggage dollies, off luggage dollies, into customs, out of customs, into mini-vans, on to airline scales, into elevators, offices, trucks. The rule here is: Do not volunteer to carry the big black case with the Lowell lighting kit in it because it will take your arm out of its socket.

On any foreign assignment, before you get your visa, before you tell your wife, before you think twice or even once, you get on the phone and book the fixer. In every foreign town, there is a squad of fixers: they find hotels, rent cars, translate; know whom to pay to get an interview with the chief of police, know how to find the commandant of the rebels and how to arrange a rendezvous; know how to get a tire fixed, a lens replaced, and the fastest route to the satellite feed-point. You must find and monopolize the best fixer. He will not steal from you, mostly, and he will not allow anyone else to steal more from you than is decent. Do not pay off the fixer until your gear is on the plane out. Nobody fades away faster than a fixer with a final pocketful of American twenties.

Don't expect an uproarious sex life. On the road you're too busy, too harassed, too sick or tired or mad at your field producer, or the assignment desk, or the assignment, or the exasperations of this benighted country to work yourself into an effective mating dance. There are exceptions to this — and one staggering exception — a technician I will call Gene, who either has a woman in every city in the world or can find one. Gene is not completely unattractive, but no stunner, either; we think (it's the subject of some round-table discussion in the hotel bar after Gene has left for the night, which he always does early, and never alone) it may be something he does with his eyes.

In many ways, this is a very silly way to make a living. There are too many nights in Holiday Inns, or pup tents in bad corners of the world, of being lonely, depressed, fed up with the road, with airports, with taxis, with being cheated and lied to and kept up past your bedtime. For most of those moments, there are antidotes: beautiful or horrible sights that bring you out of yourself and remind you why you are doing this.

In the evening, after the light goes and the cameras shut down, the crews straggle back to their hotel from the degradation and horror outside. A mile or two away, there are children with the big bellies and ginger hair of the starving, huts destroyed, medical clinics shot up and burned down. In the hotel, there is whisky and food and clean sheets.

Reporters work out the rationalizations that make them comfortable:

1• These people are used to it. Their lives that seem so horrifying to me are fulfilling by their standards. It's patronizing to think otherwise; it's condescending to feel pity.

2• I need my comforts and conveniences to do my work. My work is the real way I can offer these people some help.

Anything that makes me more comfortable is a step towards making their lives better.

None of this will give you peace of mind, but you don't really need much peace at these times because, while part of your mind is thinking: Jesus, this is horrible, most of your mind is thinking: Jesus, the pictures are going to be absolutely wonderful.

It's as true in journalism as it is in surgery or law. The professional is the human being who doesn't let his humanity distract him from his job.

After the job's done, the footage has to be sent home. In a democracy, this is easy — just call the courier. But as CBC correspondent **Sheila MacVicar** *has learned, it's more difficult in Iraq.*

During the Iran-Iraq war, we were feeding most of our material out of Iraq by satellite. This meant you had to get by the censors, as the satellites are controlled by Iraqi TV. You'd show up with your cassettes and they'd screen them. You never met the committee or heard what they thought.

They never told us what we could and could not talk about. They didn't hand out a piece of paper saying "here are our sensitivities." We just had to guess. One night they took out my entire voice-track, it just wasn't there any more. A crew from a Japanese network had their piece fed through to Tokyo without a voice track. When they asked why it was taken out, they were told: "Because we couldn't understand it."

To get around this problem, I would double-file my voice-over by telephone. The quality is not as good as satellite, but it was better than nothing. We tried to make our stand-ups as innocuous as possible so we could get them out. Beyond that, it was all *Inshallah* — God willing.

It was soon clear that we could not talk about the use of poison gas, major battle losses, or heavy casualties. You wouldn't even think about discussing the president, his popularity — or lack thereof — or his human-rights record. That would make you an automatic PNG — *persona non grata.* You'd be out on the next plane.

But it wasn't always easy to predict what the Iraqis considered sensitive. How could pictures of a café filled with old men playing backgammon and drinking tea under pictures of Saddam Hussein not be acceptable? The explanation: This is a war. Iraqi men are not sitting around drinking tea.

To make sure we didn't take home any "undesirable" footage, the Iraqis would look through all our cassettes, and then stamp each one with a seal of approval. It then became a game, as in any country with censorship, to figure out a way to smuggle "sensitive" material out.

One technique is to take the videocassettes apart and cut out the piece of tape that you want to protect. Then you take the heavy cardboard cores from a roll of gaffer tape, which no cameraperson travels without, twist the layers of cardboard open, and set the film inside. Then you replace the core inside the roll of tape.

The other trick is to submit your cassettes to the censors containing only inoffensive material. They then stamp and clear them. If you record on the first eight minutes only, you have twelve minutes to play with when you get back the cassette.

Mark Phillips *was a correspondent in Moscow for* CBS *during 1984 and 1985. He tells how he smuggled material out of pre-*Glasnost *Russia.*

To get sensitive material out of Moscow, we used the hand-carry industry: spouses of correspondents or business people would carry videotapes or editorial material with them on flights out of the country. Under the terms of the Helsinki Accords, censorship of this material is forbidden. You could even do same-day stories employing the hand-carry method because the time zones worked in our favour. The 5:00 p.m. British Airways flight to London would arrive 9:00 p.m. London time, which was only 4:00 p.m. Eastern Standard Time.

My wife did a lot of travelling during the period we were stationed in Moscow, as did all the wives. They were very popular people. We would give them a return business-class air ticket, one night in a hotel and one hundred dollars for being a good sport. It wasn't too tough to find volunteers to take a quick weekend to London.

When I was there, Moscow was the toughest general assignment I think there was. Two years seemed like ten. All foreigners live in compounds, which are under constant police guard. There's a militiaman at each entrance, checking comings and goings for our "protection." My mother came to visit from Montreal. When we passed the militiaman box at the entranceway, my mother exclaimed: "Oh! Twenty-four-hour security!"

One can assume that all apartments are bugged and all

telephone calls monitored. Early in our stay in Moscow, my wife and I were sitting in our kitchen, discussing whether or not to keep our maid. The Soviets supply you with a maid who, as we like to say, takes out *and reads* your garbage. You have the option when you first arrive to renew her contract or replace her. We thought she seemed really pleasant, but not much good at cleaning. My wife pointed to the toaster on the kitchen counter: "Look at that," she said. "It looks like it hasn't been cleaned in years." The next morning the maid arrived, took off her coat, headed directly for the toaster and started cleaning it.

CTV's **Alan Edmonds** *on why it's important to work with a cameraman who likes you:*

At the Winter Olympic Park in Calgary, the bottom third of the huge runway for one-man bobsleds is used as a sort of super-midway ride for courageous tourists. The ice-maker is turned on in the morning and, by afternoon, when it's become a bit soft and slow, you can ride the last few hundred yards for ten bucks, and navigate a couple of hair-raising bends. One run is usually enough for even the most enterprising.

I made the run to demonstrate this new way to enrich your life while in Calgary, but I made it (*a*) in the morning when the ice was fresh and fast and (*b*) for *Canadian* television. During the Winter Olympics, an NBC reporter rode the luge. They had four cameras in position: one run, four cameras. For CTV and Canadian content: one camera, four runs.

I lay prone, feet first, on the luge for a close-up. The staff were to push me out of the frame so it appeared my ride was just beginning. Cameraman Wally Corbett would then move down to the first bend and film me as I zipped by for real. He would relocate at two points farther down the course for my second and third runs. The fourth, he would film at the finish. Unhappily for the opening close-up, the staff pushed too enthusiastically and I went tearing off down the hill on an unheralded run. Unsuspecting, two men were on the track, hosing water, which becomes instant ice on the course. Mercifully, both heard my screams and leaped over the wall — a nanosecond between them and broken legs. I hit the hoses and bounced wildly up and down and from side to side, but reached the bottom with nothing dented but my courage.

Corbett, known throughout the industry for loquacious charm, said: "What'd you do that for, stupid? I wasn't ready."

After the second run (Corbett was ready and the track was clear) soundman Michael Docherty complained I panicked too loudly into his precious radio mike and told me that if I crashed and broke it, he'd sue for a replacement.

For the fifth run, Corbett set up at the end of the 100-foot strip of Astroturf at the bottom of the run. On the soft afternoon ice, you come down off the wall of the last bend between 20/30 and kph, and the Astroturf brakes the luge to a stop within a few metres. Sometimes the sticky ice stops it before it even reaches the Astroturf.

Unhappily, I was on fresh, fast ice and after four runs I had unconsciously learned something about luging. On this last run, I didn't finish at 30 kph. I shot out of the last bend at around 50 kph, whipped up on to the Astroturf, and kept on going. I crashed into Corbett and camera. Corbett, torn between survival instinct and the need to preserve his gear, jumped backwards on to the wall, but hung on to the camera. When everything stopped, my legs were wrapped around the tripod and felt broken. The camera, with Corbett clinging to it, wobbled perilously above my head, threatening to fall. The red light was still winking.

"Why?" I asked.

"You might have killed yourself. Couldn't miss that," said Corbett.

Soundman Docherty bent over and thrust his hand under my sweater. "Radio mike's okay," he said. Producer Carlyle clicked a few with his Pentax. "Production stills," he said.

As one of the CBC's *senior European correspondents,* **Patrick
Brown** *has covered many hijackings, including the brutal
1985 hijacking of* TWA *flight 847, in which one American
was murdered and forty others were held for seventeen days.
Keeping pace with terrorists is never an easy assignment.*

Hijackings are awful to cover because the hijackers fly off to
places and you can't go on their plane. It's worse than a
presidential campaign. Hijackers tend not to lay on press
planes. This is a great failing that we'll have to talk to them
about.

Quite often it becomes obvious where the hijackers are
going. Then you have to try to get a seat on a regular flight to
the same place before everybody else does. Sometimes the
American networks will charter planes, but often you have to
fly commercially.

If you guess wrong, you get lost on the way. We all had this
trouble with the *Achille Lauro*. There were correspondents
spread out around the universe. I spent three days without
sleep, chasing from one country to another, one airport to
another, without ever laying eyes on the boat.

Sometimes we are up round the clock, covering these
things, but usually they settle down into a kind of routine.
Depending on how many of you there are and whom you can
trust, you can set up a little roto [rotation system] so that if
something breaks, your system will let you know.

Everyone uses air-band radios, which pick up frequencies
between the tower and the planes. It's what everybody uses.
When you hear those conversations between the tower and
the cockpit, it's an air-band radio connected to a tape re-

corder. Sometimes the terrorists send out press communiqués, but their style tends to rely more on coming to the door of the plane and throwing out a body.

The people who argue that you are encouraging terrorism by covering it are suggesting that it is good PR to be known as somebody who blows up people, and kidnaps them, and shoots them, and tortures them. Is it really so great for the IRA to have the full scope of its activities well known? My personal feeling is that you can't not cover things. In a way, events and truth are indivisible.

On about the sixth day of the TWA hijacking , Nabih Berri, the leader of the Amal Shiites, held a press conference. We asked him if the hostages were safe, and how they were spending their time. "They are playing sports," he answered.

There being a certain amount of black humour at these things, I immediately conjured up an image of a Hostage Olympics: hang-gliding off the Shuf Mountains, grenade spoon races, that kind of thing. What he meant was that they were playing card games.

The Kuwaiti airliner that was hijacked in Bangkok in 1988 was a bit of a nightmare. First it fetched up in Cyprus and then flew off to Algeria. After days of captivity, the people were finally released. As they came down the steps, there was general pandemonium, screaming and yelling, and reporters' questions. In the crush, I was separated from our camera, which meant I was unable to record one of the best exchanges I've ever heard. A reporter asked one of the hostages: "I suppose after this terrible ordeal, you'll be very relieved to be reunited with your family and your loved ones." And he said: "Well, no, as a matter of fact, I won't. I told my wife I was going to Mecca for the pilgrimage and now I've been caught on a plane coming back from Bangkok." This man was in deep trouble. If you're going to misbehave, it's very important not to get hijacked.

The Journal's **Linden MacIntyre** *abandoned all shame in the pursuit of an important interview.*

While we were in El Salvador doing a piece on the 1984 elections, we were having trouble pinning down President Duarte for an interview. He was ducking us all over the place. Finally, we noted in the newspaper that his mother had died. We located the church in San Salvador his mother was "resting" in, and we just hung around the coffin until Napoleon Duarte showed up. Duarte paid his last respects to Mom, and then, as he walked away, we pounced. "Mr. Duarte!" we said. "We're with the CBC. On behalf of all Canadians, we want to convey our sympathy to you. Now, whattaya say about an interview?" The temerity of our approach impressed him. As bodyguards were reaching inside their coat pockets, he said, "Okay. Come around to the office after the funeral." We did, and got our interview.

Former ABC correspondent **Hilary Brown** *tells us how a clever disguise and nerves of steel can help win a story.*

In reporting foreign news, you constantly run up against officials who are trying to stop you from showing what's really happening. When you battle these people to get the story out, you aren't thinking about the danger involved, you're thinking: "Wow! Are they ever going to love this back home."

I was carried by that sense of exhilaration when I was sent to Africa in the late seventies to cover a rebellion in Katanga province [now called Shaba], in what is now Zaire. We were dispatched to Kinshasa, the capital. We stayed at the Intercontinental and inhaled that delicious Bouquet d'Afrique — a not totally unpleasant combination of oily food, sweat, and dust. It's a distinctive smell. Pungent.

We found ourselves stuck in Kinshasa several hundred miles from Katanga. The government had closed the roads and air routes so that no journalist could get down south to cover this war.

We figured the only way to get there would be to stow away on one of the military transport planes going in and out of Katanga. So, the crew and I went out and bought some army fatigues. The best time to do things like this is between one and five in the morning when people are really tired and security is likely to be more lax, and, dressed in our fatigues, we went out to the military airport at midnight. We hung around watching until about 4:00 a.m., when a Hercules transport plane on the runway was being loaded up. Of course, assuming it was going to Katanga was sort of insane, but you are driven to such madness because of the fiercely competitive nature of the business.

We sauntered onto the runway and climbed on board. The couple of pilots, lolling around the cockpit, didn't seem to care. The cargo happened to be petrol. If we crashed, we would be very charred witnesses. It didn't make it any easier that the pilots kept throwing their burning cigarette butts into the back of the plane.

About 5:00 a.m., they pulled up the bay, revved the engines, and we took off. Because there was tremendous activity at the airport with all the supplies coming in when we landed, nobody bothered about us. I was able to put together a coherent story. Then we found a pigeon, a person you can trust to take the stuff back and drop it off, at the Intercontinental Hotel. We hunkered down and filed stories every day for a week to the great fury of the press corps in Kinshasa, who couldn't figure out how we did it.

*The reports **Ann Medina** filed out of the Middle East in the
late seventies and early eighties for the CBC were broadcast
worldwide, informing and moving audiences around the
globe. Her coolness in the midst of all the violence and terror
left an indelible impression in the memories of most viewers.*

My first trip to the Middle East was in 1977. I had been in
intense things in the States — gang wars and riots — but
never a war. My producer had never been abroad before,
except with the prime minister. It was also all new for the
cameraman and soundman. It's hard to believe that they sent
a woman correspondent, with the greenest team imaginable,
into one of the most ridiculously insane situations in the
world, but they did it. And what's more incredible is that I did
it. I was a fool.

Later, I would go back only with the most experienced
crew and producer. It's too dangerous otherwise. There are
so many things you better know that I just didn't. The fact
that roads were mined. Or, the press-card shuffle. Each faction demanded a different press card. You had to know how
to identify each faction by their uniforms to avoid showing
them the wrong card.

You'd get up at 5:30 a.m., and by 6:30 a.m. someone from
one of the networks would be already back in the Commodore lobby, shaking his head saying he will never go out
there again. There was no control on the streets.

The PLO made you come by their office to pick up your
press card. But just to go to that office was . . . well, it took all
of your courage. The streets were full of young crazies out of

control — fighting, pushing, shoving, beating people up. Our soundman had a gun clicked in his back. And that was just to get the press pass. A press pass — what a civilized concept! The truth is, after all the chaos of getting there and back, this press pass meant bugger all.

My press pass became a photo of Arafat and me arm-in-arm. It certainly wouldn't work with everybody but, for the right people, the photo was magic. I carried it around and waved it when things got too hot. Much more effective than an official press pass or even an aide. Of course, those poses actually make you cringe, especially when other people see them and say: "Oh! So you were a good buddy of Arafat's." Which, of course, you're not.

On every story, you measure the risk. Sometimes you decide it's not worth it. Every move is thought out in advance. If I go down here, which road can I leave from? Who controls that road? Are they strong-enough to hold it? If I get stuck in that town, how long am I going to be stuck? Is there a building with big-enough walls that I'll be safe in? Can I get any pictures if I'm stuck there? You just ask and ask and ask.

Whenever you drove down a road and the car in front of you turned around, *you* also turned around. You may have no idea why they turned around, but you always play it safe. If you ever wanted to botch up another network, you'd make sure they were driving behind you, and then you would turn back. They would have no idea why you did it, but they would do it, too. Then, of course, you would try again later, hoping they had given up.

But while we played little tricks on each other, we also shared all our information. You would save a few little gems for yourself, but never if those gems involved safety. Every-body shares. You do it because you're going to get as much as you give. It will save your life sometimes. It's not that anyone is being generous; you're being very selfish. You are finding out how to keep your crew together. It's open season on misleading people, but not when it involves safety. I would never send someone down a road for a great story if I didn't know what was down that road.

In many ways, I believe the worst part of that assignment was what we put our parents and mates through. They don't know what's going on, and, of course, they're worried. There comes a point when you just can't put them through it any more. One time my brother called me before I left for a trip I was petrified about. He bawled me out, called me an idiot, which was his wonderful way of telling me that he loved me. My mother was great. She just said: "Well, that's fine. Tell us when you get back and be careful."

Alison Smith *shares her most reliable method of scooping:*

After the whole Sinclair Stevens kerfuffle blew up in the House, Stevens went to his farm, north of Toronto. A large portion of the press corps followed. We all drove around his acreage, looking for ways to get closer to the house, but it was impossible. The house was safely positioned on top of a hill, so we were staked out at the bottom of the road.

It was a nice summer day — not the worst stakeout we've ever done — and we just waited everybody out. That's the standard way to get a scoop. You just wait until everyone else gets tired and goes home. I telephoned from the car phone and said, "Mr. Stevens, we are the only ones left. This is *The National*. Don't you think you'd like to come and talk to us?" I reassured him he wouldn't have to face the media hordes.

We got this wonderful picture of him coming from his house in his little pick-up truck with his farm manager, the dust curling out from the back of the truck. He came down and, leaning over his gate, gave us an interview. It was great to get on the phone to the office and say: "We got him!" He didn't tell us anything new, but we did get him. All it took was a wait from nine in the morning until six at night. Simple.

It is during the scrum, when reporters push and shove microphones, cameras, notebooks and their own bodies into the faces of politicians, that reporters get most of their official, "on-the-record" contact with politicians. CBC's **Wendy Mesley** *insists no other Canadian politician is quite as adroit at handling such orchestrated chaos as is our prime minister.*

One of the best things about being a reporter on the Hill is scrums. I love them — I wear high heels and I spike anyone who gets in the way. Mulroney prefers the staircase for his scrums. We think it is so that he can look down on us. Also it gives him control. He can avoid being shot by a camera lens three inches from his nose. His routine is to ignore us, start up the stairs, and, if he hears a question he likes, turn around — far enough away to look presidential — and answer. When it gets on to a topic he doesn't like, he simply walks away. He's learned how to walk away looking dignified.

Some of the cameramen have been around for five, ten, even twenty years. Their faces are very familiar to all the politicians. Sometimes the cameramen are better known than the reporters. They know the biggest audiences are behind Larry Brown, *The National*'s cameraman, so they play to him.

*In October 1983, a coup overthrew the Communist
government of Grenada; Prime Minster Maurice Bishop was
murdered. Within days, the United States invaded the
island, ostensibly to defend a handful of American medical
students. Fifteen thousand troops "saved" the students and
happened to leave behind a sympathetic, non-Communist
government. Like hundreds of journalists from around the
world,* The Journal's **Terrence McKenna** *attempted to
cover an invasion the Americans wanted to keep
strictly private.*

The first radio bulletins of the American invasion of Grenada
sounded like silly rumours, but, within a couple of hours, I
was climbing on to a Lear jet with camerman Jean-Guy Nault,
heading for the Caribbean. We had the odd idea that we
might be able to just land at the Grenada Airport and go to
work.

The Americans were diverting all non-military flights to
Barbados, and they were not allowing journalists on their
military flights. So, we were stuck with hundreds of other
reporters in Barbados.

Then we got a hot tip that a Canadian military plane was
going in to evacuate Canadian citizens. We grabbed our
equipment, dodged past security, and ran for all we were
worth . . . leaping through the rear cargo door of a Canadian
Hercules transport just seconds before the aircraft started
rolling. The Canadian Armed Forces personnel on board
told us it would be very dangerous, that we would likely be
under fire at the Grenada Airport as the Canadian evacuees

were pulled on board, and that we should stay out of the way. But we were not worried about any of that. We had outwitted the U.S. censors and were about to get an international exclusive! Wrong. As we circled Grenada, the Canadian pilot was told to "buzz off" by U.S. military air-traffic control. Anyone getting saved was going to be saved by the U.S. army.

Back with the pack in Barbados, we decided to sneak on to Grenada by boat. We chartered a small plane to Saint Vincent, where we hired a filthy, old fishing boat. This should do the trick, we thought, until a couple of F-14 Tomcat fighter jets circled the boat a few times. We were hiding below — nobody here but us old fishermen. Minutes later, a U.S. Navy helicopter dropped a flare in front of our bow, a signal to cut our engines and stop immediately. They advised us by bullhorn that this was "a quarantined war zone." As we deliberated the possiblity of pretending ignorance, a U.S. Navy destroyer appeared and asked us to identify ourselves. We owned up to being Canadian journalists intending to land on Grenada. The Navy said this was a war zone and that we could not do that.

I argued that I knew of no international law that allowed the U.S. Government to interfere with our passage through international waters. At that point, the captain came on the radio, saying that his orders were to prevent us from landing on Grenada, using whatever force was required.

That night, in a bar on Union Island in the Grenadines, the hot topic of conversation was the one guy who'd made it: a *Newsweek* photographer who'd eluded the U.S. Navy cordon in a small speedboat. The next day we tracked down the speedboat owner, a young American who ran a scuba business on Palm Island. After he'd landed the *Newsweek* man, his boat was stopped by a U.S. Navy destroyer. He protected the identity of his passenger until he found himself face down on the destroyer deck with a boot on his head and the muzzle of an M-16 pressed against his neck. When they clicked off the safety, he talked. I allowed as how he was probably not eager for a return voyage with us. "Hell sure, I'll take you," he said. "Fuck 'em, if they can't take a joke."

Soon we were shooting across the water in a little Boston Whaler with two 120-hpr engines on the back. Our hopes surged until one of the engines broke down and we had to limp all the way back to Palm Island.

At five the next morning, we were rattled out of our beds by the roar of passing F-14s. The Americans were conducting a supplementary invasion of Curaçao, which belongs to Grenada, to mop up any remaining resistance. We were now allowed to proceed by boat to Grenada. In a few hours, we were all there being mercilessly razzed on the telephone from home office because we would have reached Grenada sooner had we waited with all the other journalists in Barbados.

Former Journal *correspondent* **Ann Medina** *describes the delicate art of bribery.*

Everyone jokes about bribery in this business. But it is something you just have to do. There are times when you have to pay to get visas, or equipment across borders, or to make things happen in six rather than twenty hours. Canadians may like to deny that we do it, but that's bullshit. We may pay one hundred dollars when the Americans have to pay two thousand or ten thousand dollars, but we all do it.

In 1984, I wanted to get into Syria to do features rather than straight news stories. I was surprised but delighted when I received a telex from the man in Syria responsible for the foreign press. This man's name was Doctor Zaboob. We never did learn what Zaboob was a doctor of. Dr. Zaboob was prepared to do his utmost to make our visit to Syria productive. However, there was a small condition. We must bring along a meat grinder, specifically a Moulinex meat grinder, as a token of our appreciation.

It wasn't hard to figure out: Doctor Zaboob had a wife at home who regularily wailed: "Whaaaa! I want a meat grinder! I have to make chopped meat all the time! You get me a meat grinder!" Poor old Doctor Zaboob had to follow through, with a little help from the Canadian Broadcasting Corporation.

In Syria, I met, every morning, with Dr. Zaboob to learn what I was and was not allowed to film that day. A long and arduous task. I held back the meat grinder until the end of our stay when I needed a key interview with Foreign Minister Sharra. Then the back and forth began. "Well, Miss Medina, have you got the meat grinder?" "Oh! I left it in my hotel!" I said. "I meant to bring it in. I'm sorry, but what about that interview?"

Only after our interview with Sharra did Zaboob get his blender. What gets you access? Sometimes something as kooky as a kitchen appliance.

CTV's **Jim Reed** *on journalistic plagarism:*

There is a sleazy side to journalism. I have seen so many cases — especially in the Middle East — where the reporter doesn't feel like going out so he will interview another reporter who did, then file it himself. You take the film from another network and telephone in the voice-over. A lot more of that goes on than people realize. If you trust the person who's telling you what happened, that's one thing. But the possibility that person made up the facts is real, especially in a conflict where nobody knows the truth. The truth becomes whatever anybody says it is. This is why I don't believe a lot of what I see on TV. I trust what I do. But the viewer never knows what's been edited out.

CBC's **Patrick Brown** *on the wisdom of cultivating friendly relations with the competition:*

When I was reporting on Quebec politics between 1976 and 1980, the guys from *The New York Times* would hang around for a few days for a story I'd been beavering away on for years. It's rather fun to have them pick your brains, then go away, write it up — and get it all wrong. It's fun. It's non-threatening and an investment.

Journalists help each other out because we all know we're in deep trouble. And if we're not in deep trouble today, we're going to be in deep trouble tomorrow. We are competing in a way, but it's such an unpredictable business where so many things can go wrong that you help on the assumption that everything comes back.

*The sportsmanship that makes the process work is
occasionally abused. When* CTV*'s* **Pamela Wallin** *was in El
Salvador to cover the civil war, she found her famous* ABC
colleague a little too willing to lean on her.

We were down in El Salvador for a few days. We have a co-
operative arangement with ABC, which has a permanent oper-
ation in Salvador. In the morning, we sat down with their
producer and agreed to divide reporting duties for the day.
They would do military exercises, we would do a refugee
camp, and we'd exchange tape at the end of the day. They got
the easier job, of course, because they were only taking
pictures.

That night we went out for a late dinner with our American friends. I knew they had liked our pictures because the
reporter had called me that afternoon to say he was really
pleased with them and could I tell him more about them.
Naively, I blathered on about how disturbing it was to see this
refugee camp. I described the squalor, the misery. I told him
the stench had burned my nostrils.

After dinner, the editor invited us to look at the piece they
cut. I went up to the ABC edit suite, and there on the screen
was ABC reporter John Quinones, who hadn't even gone out
of the hotel that day. ABC reporters who are on the road for
more than two weeks are entitled to conjugal visits. The
network had flown his girlfriend down and they had spent
the day together by the pool. Quinones was giving a first-
person account of his visit to the refugee camp. He said it was
incredibly disturbing. The stench had burned his nostrils.

A little airport espionage is all part of the day's work for
CBC's **Terry Milewski**.

When Trudeau took his famous walk in the blizzard, I was on
my way home from a week with Salvadorean guerrillas and
was told: "You better get back here quick. We're calling
everyone back to Canada."

In the Miami airport, I saw CTV reporter Jim Munson
sitting on a flight bag. He affably told me where he was going,
although, since he was sitting at the Air Jamaica counter, it
wasn't hard to deduce. It took me a moment to make the
connection: John Turner must be in Jamaica. I got on the
telephone. The CBC said: "You better get on that plane, too."

I regrouped the crew that had been with me in El Salvador
for the flight to Jamaica. And I remember paying my driver a
little extra not to tell Munson's driver where in Jamaica we
were going. Neither of us knew where Turner — who was
potentially the next prime minister of Canada — was spending his holiday, but we each had to find out and get an
interview.

The two of us played cat-and-mouse. My Ottawa office had
a hot tip for me on Turner's whereabouts. I followed it, and it
turned out to be wrong. CTV had got it right, and Munson got
the first interview. I got to Turner only after Munson was
safely heading out on the last flight of the day.

To save my career from going down the toilet, we had to get
our Turner interview out to Miami that night before the start
of the *National News*. We chartered a jet that we had to push
across the tarmac to the fuel truck and gas it up, as the truck

driver was stoned on ganja.

By this time it was dark and we couldn't get permission to fly over Cuba, so we had to fly around it, losing more time. Eventually we got to Miami, but customs wanted to take a little time with two unshaven white guys off a chartered jet from Jamaica, with no luggage except some videotape in a briefcase.

The cameraman who had been working very hard, in both Nicaragua and El Salvador, had in his pocket some yellow pills he'd bought in a Salvadorean pharmacy. He had said to the druggist, "*Ariba, Ariba* (up, up)," and received these pills, which were of great interest to the customs man in Miami who didn't care how late we were for our feed.

The customs man took the pills out of the bag, and emptied them into a little plastic bottle with a fluid inside to see what colour they would go. I went white and the cameraman went red. But the crystals went blue — which was the right colour. We were now twenty minutes from show time. We were scheduled to file with the help of the NBC bureau, who were watching from the other side of the barrier. The NBC driver ran twenty-two red lights and we got Turner on the air.

I suspect that Jim Munson wished he had pretended he was just going on a holiday. But it was he who saw me first and said, "Hi." I'd have hidden behind a newspaper.

CTV *cameraman* **Jim Mercer** *insists that good journalists always keep their shirts on.*

Whenever I hear the unique "thwack, thwack, thwack" sound of a helicopter hovering just above me, it triggers a memory thirty years old. Newfoundland's illustrious premier Joey Smallwood had renamed the magnificent Hamilton Falls in Labrador "Churchill Falls." Let's forget for the moment that this move was motivated by a desire to impress the Rothschild Bank in London, where Joey was looking for money, and that these phenomenal falls, which were twice as high as Niagara, would disappear when Joey's power generators were built.

This day's glorious event was to feature a quick visit by Sir Winston Churchill's grandson, Winston. News and documentary film crews were transported by truck over a very rough road and dropped at a barren location near the Falls. As we waited for Mr. Churchill's arrival, a sudden rain squall hit. "I have an idea," said a young Henry Champ. "Let's put the rain covers on the cameras and put our clothes in the empty camera cases. The rain is bound to stop before the VIPs arrive, and we won't have to look like a bunch of drowned rats." We all thought this was a great idea and quickly stuffed our clothes into the waterproof camera cases.

But, alas, before the rain stopped, we heard the "thwack, thwack, thwack" of a helicopter skimming over the nearest hill. Decisions, decisions. What to do? Run for our clothes and miss Mr. Churchill's landing, or run for the cameras and save our jobs. Out of cowardice rather than valour, we ran for

the cameras. That's why our pictures showed a rather confused Mr. Churchill alighting from the chopper. I guess he
wondered why nobody had briefed him that hardy Canadian
crews worked nude in the summer.

CLOSE ENCOUNTERS

Much of the pleasure of the news profession is in rubbing shoulders with the powerful, flirting with the glamorous, cajoling the kooky.

News is often personalized because of the tendency among journalists and viewers to identify issues with individuals. After the dull details of the Free Trade Agreement are long forgotten (do you remember the schedule of tariff reductions on plastic gaskets?), memories of our negotiator Simon Reisman flourish.

The reporters who get to meet the world's most colourful characters may not like everyone they encounter, but they're usually glad to have been in the same room.

When the frosty Mrs. Thatcher came to town, CTV's **Pamela Wallin** *tried her best to de-ice her. On the other hand, Simon Reisman was an explosion to be contained.*

Margaret Thatcher

When Margaret Thatcher was here in the early 1980s, I did a live interview with her from the British High Commission for *Canada* AM. We arrived at five in the morning to prepare the set. Because it was a live show, we insisted that Mrs. Thatcher arrive ten minutes before airtime for logistical reasons.

We were sitting in these chairs and she would not deal with me. She would not anwer my questions. She was barking orders to all and sundry. She had the entire set rearranged when she came down, saying it was "just *not* acceptable."

So we moved everything around in a circle, and then put it back exactly the way it was because that was the only way it could be. But now she felt better because at least she had created a stir. She made everyone jump — which was what she was after.

It was post-Falklands, so there was a lot to talk about. I was trying to break the ice and she wouldn't play. Then, half-consciously but half not, I looked at my monitor and said to the make-up artist: "I think Mrs. Thatcher needs some more cheeks, she's looking pale." Mrs. Thatcher instantly looked at the monitor and said: "Oh! You are quite right!" And over came the make-up lady and put on more blush.

From then on, Mrs. Thatcher changed completely. She became totally charming and we chatted nicely. Somehow this small show on my part — that I really cared about how she looked — changed her. She did look a bit pale, but I don't think that was my real motivation. It was a desperate manoeuvre. But it worked, even on a woman who has a reputation for having ice water running through her veins. I had a different view of her after that — not her politics, but her. In a tiny episode like that, you can see a human being in there after all.

Simon Reisman

Reisman was out of public life for fifteen years and didn't understand the scrum. He would come out of all those endless free-trade meetings and announce: "I have nothing to say. I am simply not going to talk to the press." Forty-five minutes later we're begging: "Simon! Please don't give us any more! We're running out of tape!"

He has a wonderfully large ego, twice the size of his body. He would come out of the meetings and love all the attention, though he was instructed not to speak to anyone. So he said: "No I'm not going to speak to anyone," and then would stand there for forty-five minutes and do it.

He would be that way on *Question Period*, too. He was always crazy in those interviews. Television hadn't been a real factor in his earlier negotiations, nor did he really speak to the press much when he was a deputy-minister. So I went through the program's format with him, explaining that we would have commercial breaks, and that we were going to try to cover as many issues as possible in the limited time.

Coming up to the final minutes of the interview, I said: "We are quickly running out of time, so I want to ask you this one last point . . ." He starts in with a very long-winded answer, and, of course, I have to cut him off. Reisman was startled. "What are you doing? What do you mean? I'm not done yet!" So, we faded to commercial with Simon Reisman pounding the table and yelling, "I'm not done!"

During eight years at The Journal, **Barbara Frum** *has discovered that it's the really cranky guests she remembers most vividly. The one exception was former United States president Jimmy Carter whose abject niceness was a story in itself.*

Jimmy Carter

We went to Atlanta to interview Jimmy Carter the winter after he left office. Carter had rented the top floor of the federal government building in Atlanta. He was working on his memoirs. When you entered the building, there was a roster of tenants and a plaque that read "President Jimmy Carter."

Now, I appreciate that in the United States you never lose a title once you've got it, but there was something so poignant about seeing his name spelled out so grandly on the roster of this banal, impersonal public building.

When you got off the elevator on the top floor, there was a plaque on the wall that read "President Jimmy Carter." On his door another announced "Office of President Jimmy Carter." Wherever there was a blank space, there was another brass plaque to remind you. He was so happy to be interviewed — we could have stayed a week. I'm sure that when he left the White House he thought no one would ever speak to him again.

CBC anchor Peter Mansbridge with David Halton: "If we ever showed everything we have access to, people would be really upset."

CBC-Regina correspondent Mansbridge in 1976 at the Great Wall of China: "I was in the early days of realizing that I was losing my hair and sought solutions at the Shanghai herbal clinic."

The Journal's Bill Cameron atop a camel in east Jerusalem: "In many ways, this is a very silly way to make a living."

CBC reporter Terry Milewski wisely shielding his head in Beirut: "The problem of journalism anywhere is that access becomes so precious, you have to be nice to the people who mete it out."

CTV's Mike Duffy posing at the Toronto site of the 1988 economic summit: "Relationships between the press and politicians are today much more intense and much more adversarial."

Wendy Mesley of CBC's Ottawa bureau: "One of the best things about being a reporter on the Hill is scrums. I wear high heels and I spike anyone who gets in the way."

Former *Journal* reporter Ann Medina: "On every story you measure the risk. Sometimes you decide it's not worth it. You just ask and ask and ask."

The Journal's Barbara Frum with Paul McCartney: "I was struck by his presumption that any female would be water on the pavement before him. I giggled in embarrassment to be cast as a groupie."

The late Clark Todd in a photo
taken shortly before his death in
1983. He was killed on
assignment in Lebanon.

CTV's Craig Oliver in Managua,
Nicaragua. To stay alive in
Central America, "Use the
technique I employ
increasingly – don't go!"

CBC's Ottawa correspondent
Don Newman: "Younger
reporters who want everything
on the record are kidding
themselves."

Newsworld's Alison Smith:
"The standard way to get a
scoop? You just wait until
everyone else gets tired and goes
home."

Doug Small bureau chief of Global News, holds a copy of the leaked 1989 federal budget: "It just dropped into my lap."

The Journal's Brian Stewart covering famine in Sudan: "I had a very clear objective – to alert the outside world, and quickly."

Linden MacIntyre of *The Journal* with Israeli troops in southern Lebanon: "Journalists survive by carefully erecting shields of reserve around themselves."

A *Journal* crew films in Central America. The challenge is to get close enough to danger to seem authoritative, but not so close as to need surgery.

Paul McCartney

I hate interviewing stars. They bore me solid. I guess I don't empathize with them enough. They act as though talking about themsleves and selling their film or album is the biggest imposition in the world. I may love their movies or their music — I just don't care about them.

Big show-biz stars like Paul McCartney operate with their own camera crews. You show up with your cassette, your cassette gets slapped into their camera, and you've got five minutes' access — and no more — to do your interview. The result is usually a verbal form of extruded plastic.

In this instance, we travelled to New York and agreed to be last in line if we could record our own interview. McCartney had done some interviews in the morning, and then he and his wife, Linda, went to the Palm Court Room at the Plaza for lunch. They decided to have a long lunch. A two-hour lunch. They couldn't care less that they had twenty-five journalists waiting for them upstairs. And we were last.

I was quite irritated by the time he finally arrived with a photographer in tow. His little gig was that, before you sat down to interview him, all visiting interviewers got their picture taken with Paul McCartney. He put his arm around you and his cameraman snapped your picture, which he would autograph and mail to you later. Of course, everyone on The Journal crew wanted a picture with him, too. So there's another long wait while a million Polaroids and automatic flash lights go off. Then the autographs. This performance was much better than the interview.

I was struck by his presumption that any female would be

water on the pavement before him. He just presumed that. I giggled in embarrassment to be cast as a groupie. It wasn't a very good interview. I thought he was extremely pretty, but too in love with himself.

Jeane Kirkpatrick

When Jeane Kirkpatrick was the American ambassador to the United Nations, she kept us waiting for an interview like nobody had ever kept us waiting, even Paul McCartney. We flew to New York very early because the interview had to air the same night. There had been endless negotiations with Kirkpatrick for the interview. We committed not to edit her. We would do it exactly to time, recording the same number of minutes we would play on air.

Kirkpatrick was in the U.S. mission when we arrived, involved in another meeting. Usually when someone important keeps you waiting, you are told why your time has been pre-empted and given some idea of how long a wait it will be. In this case, the attitude was indifference — we don't know when she's coming or even where she is.

After several hours, an aide asked for the make-up artist to accompany him to another floor to make her up. She wouldn't come down without make-up. I proposed to this aide that I would like to come up with our make-up artist just to say hello and tell her what I had in mind, so she'd be comfortable in the interview.

I thought I was doing her a favour, but no one soothes snappish Jeane Kirkpatrick. I suspect she believes that being snappish makes her seem impressive. It was immediately clear that the aide was so frightened of her, he was not about to arrive before her with me in tow.

When Kirkpatrick eventually came down, we were told to be in our places, and ready to roll because she was in a hurry. And then she came in, sat down, and turned her face to me. Her first words were: "That's a pretty blouse. And that's a pretty pin." And I thought: Oh swell, girl talk! Is that supposed to be disarming? I would have thought that her first logical sentence might have been: "I am sorry to have kept you waiting for two and a half hours."

Paul Simon

I just loved the *Graceland* album and worked very hard on my interview with Paul Simon. He's terminally shy. My producer was really in love with him, and she was very disheartened when she saw he had a hairpiece. I didn't notice it, but I wasn't looking at him the way she was.

Before and after the interview, he was wonderful. He told us a charming story about performing at the Apollo Theater in Harlem on tour for *Graceland*. He was being honoured by the theatre and it was a great moment for him. But, as he told us, when it came time for him to get on stage, the master of ceremonies launched into an enormous, womped-up introduction, which ended with: "Here he is. The man you've all been waiting for. The great, the incomparable — NEIL SIMON!"

We were charmed by this story but, when we went to do the interview, he was like a monk who has taken a vow of silence. He wouldn't say a word. Finally, I just said to him: "Don't you know how much we all love this album?" But he couldn't put the praise anywhere. It couldn't nourish him. He was full of angst. I liked him and I liked the album, but he was quite miserable, and he was taking his misery out on me.

He answered in yeses and nos. I ran out of questions quickly and quit. There's just a limit to the number of one-word answers you can run in a row. Two or three, okay, but then you need a longer one.

Failures like that used to kill me, now they make me laugh. After a while you just say to yourself, how bad can it get? You go for your personal worst. A bad interview isn't amusing, but a grotesquely appalling one is. You pass a line when enough good has gone by, you can tolerate a little bad.

During his tenure as CTV'*s Washington correspondent,*
Craig Oliver *got his chance to interview the world's most*
affable big guy.

I like riding and, so, before I did an interview with Reagan, we talked about riding. He may have been president of the United States, but this is not a guy you discuss policy with.

We talked about McClelland saddles, developed for the U.S. Cavalry during the Civil War. Reagan had been a cavalryman, so we had a good talk about the cavalry, which wasn't abolished until 1942. He was very charming.

Then he started telling me about his desk, which was made of wood discovered by an American expedition that had gone out to find Franklin, but then we had to do the interview. When it was over, Reagan said: "Now, don't leave yet. I want to tell you the story about the desk." His aides were all anxious because, obviously, he has other things to do. But he goes into this long story about the ship that went up to join the Franklin search. You got the feeling he would have stayed and chatted you up all day. His aides were chomping at the bit. Finally they said: "Mr. President, you have another meeting." He just rolled his eyes and said: "I've got to go . . . ."

Warren Beatty failed to make Journal *correspondent*
Susan Reisler *swoon. His interview didn't reach*
rapturous heights either.

Somewhere along the line, at *Sunday Morning* radio, they
decided I needed a break from politics. Warren Beatty had
just released a new movie, *Heaven Can Wait.* Now, I like
movies, but *Heaven Can Wait* was not high on my list.
Nevertheless the producers of the arts section of *Sunday
Morning* asked me if I wanted to go interview Warren Beatty.
I thought, what am I going to interview Warren Beatty about?
And after I saw the film, I felt there was even less to talk about.
But I knew that Warren Beatty had some political blood in
him, so I could talk to him about something interesting.

So we sit down at this little desk. Mark Starowicz has this
philosophy about where you have to hold the microphone. It
has to be three inches from a man's nose. By holding a
microphone really close, you create a sense of intimacy. The
background, whether it is an air-conditioner or anything else,
is very much in the background. People talk softer and you
can hear them clearly. So, here I am really close to Warren
Beatty. But obviously I had the wrong tone and the wrong
questions. The whole thing didn't go very well.

It could have developed into something interesting if he
allowed himself to talk. He didn't give anything away. I had to
pull out every word. He wouldn't talk about politics or
anything that I thought was interesting. Finally, we decided
enough of this torture. Finished, thank you, goodbye.

He walked me to the elevator. And I asked — I don't know

why I didn't ask this on tape — "So what's your next project?"

"I'm thinking about making a film of John Reed's book."

"*Ten Days that Shook the World?*"

This is a remarkable book about the Soviet revolution! We could have had a great conversation about why he had chosen such a book. I knew there was a brain up there! But by the time I found that out, I was standing in the elevator.

I was scared to go back to Toronto and admit failure, but my producer said, "Don't worry, nobody else has gotten a good interview out of Warren Beatty either." He was stubborn and he wasn't going to give anything. There wasn't enough material on tape to run the interview, so I couldn't even use the material that I had collected in the elevator. Now, whenever I see anyone else interview him, I have very mixed feelings. I feel really sorry for the person doing the interview because I know how hard it is. On the other hand, I'm glad each time he doesn't give anything away because I think to myself: Ha! That interviewer didn't do any better than I did!

Frank Sinatra's charm is legendary but proved a myth for
The Journal's **Bruce Garvey.**

The scene is the pretentiously named Casa Pacifica, the so-
called California White House. It's a sprawling stucco bun-
galow in San Clemente — lots of California Spanish tile —
where Nixon will introduce special guest Leonid Brezhnev to
his version of the cream of American society. Nixon crony
Bebe Rebozo is there, presumably representing the capitalist
system, and there's a strong Hollywood contingent. In the
receiving line that snakes around the backyard swimming
pool is one Francis Albert Sinatra. The fact that Sinatra had
recently made headlines by calling prominent columnist
Maxine Cheshire "a two-dollar hooker" in a popular Washington hotel restaurant is clearly a plus in this company. In a
tiny velvet-roped enclosure are six privileged reporters and,
by a geo-political happenstance, I'm one of them.

Spotting Sinatra, UPI's White House correspondent Helen
Thomas yells out from behind our restraining rope, "Hey,
Frank! What did you say to Maxine Cheshire?"

Old Blue Eyes scowls and the redoubtable Ms. Thomas
ploughs on.

"Did you say it? Did you call her that?"

Sinatra takes a step towards the enclosure and snarls,
"Nah. And I don't make no comments to three-dollar broads
like you either."

In his capacity as The National's *correspondent responsible for all events north of Baffin Island,* **Whit Fraser** *encountered few members of Canada's glamour-set. Nonetheless, somewhere near the North Pole, he did stumble upon one of the world's five richest men.*

Billionaire real-estate developer Albert Reichman was one of the sponsors of the 1988 Canadian-Soviet ski expedition that crossed the Arctic ice cap from the Soviet Union to Ellesmere Island. It was the first such journey, and our crew met the skiers at the North Pole.

Reichman decided to come, too, and he joined us in Frobisher Bay. The plan was to fly to Resolute, refuel at the weather station on Ellesmere Island and at the military establishment in Alert before finally flying to a Soviet ice station that drifts with the Arctic ice pack about fifty miles from the North Pole.

On the plane, Larry Brown, my cameraman from the Parliament Hill bureau, and Reichman were engaged in deep conversation, although it was clear that Larry didn't know who his companion was. Talking amiably to strangers was never a problem for Brown. He's one of the most congenial and likeable people in the business.

At Resolute, we had an hour's refuelling stop. Reichman was trying to use the pay phone in the cramped terminal building, but he had no change. He quietly spoke to Larry, who cheerfully handed over some coins. Reichman returned to the telephone.

A few minutes later, Reichman approached a group of us standing in the waiting room. He pressed some change into Brown's hand, saying matter-of-factly, "I had better pay you back. I don't want to lose my good credit." By that time, Brown had figured out whom he had been been dealing with and realized, to his delight, that he had just participated in the financial big leagues.

Jesse Jackson's sermons may be fiery, but as Washington-based CBC *cameraman* **David Hall** *remembers, he makes a lousy travelling companion.*

I was the CBC cameraman on Jesse Jackson's campaign plane — for a brief time. There was never any food or booze on the plane. No food for budget reasons, and no booze because Jesse is ostensibly a minister. (You did get Coke or Diet Coke, served at room temperature in a Styrofoam cup.) Jesse also forbade smoking. When we boarded the plane, the guys from NBC warned us that they had been reduced to scavaging for Twinkies at every stop, as Jackson neglected to schedule eating breaks for the TV crews. At night we'd land in small towns and stay at hotels without kitchens. You couldn't even get sandwiches made for the next day. We were always hungry.

Jackson was never on time for any event. It was a chronic thing. I'm not talking about fifteen minutes. He would start off every day late and it would snowball, so that, by the end of the day, it was out of control. At one rainy outdoor rally in the Bronx, he arrived two hours late. People were angry. Once, when he was supposed to be at a rally in Atlanta, he was still at another meeting two hundred miles away. That's the way he ran his schedule. And there was never any explanation.

The most annoying part, however, was the way his handlers treated us. We were rushed everywhere. We'd get piled on to a school bus and hauled off to a church or someplace. Everthing was hurry, hurry, hurry. You'd rush in like mad, set everything up, and then wait and wait for him to show.

After the event, his handlers would yell at us: "Okay! Let's go! Got to rush! We're late . . ." So we would frantically tear everything apart, load on to the school bus — once I had to jump into it while it was moving — and drive out to the airport. We would be herded on to the airplane and then sit there for two hours while Jesse was God-knows-where, doing God-knows-what. After a few days, while waiting on the steamy tarmac of San Antonio Airport on a hot, rainy, humid day, we decided to give the campaign the hook, get a meal, and go back to Washington.

If reporters seem a tad aggressive in their efforts to nab, harass, and cajole harried cabinet ministers as they flee the corridors of Parliament Hill, it is because they cannot count on other opportunities for exchange. **Pamela Wallin** *of* CTV *reveals the remarkable challenge of getting a politician to talk.*

It's very difficult to get politicians to come on television in Canada. Press secretaries on Parliament Hill believe it is their duty to keep the press away from their ministers. The concept is really twisted. It usually takes weeks of negotiations to get a minister on the show. You phone every day, five days a week, three weeks running.

Sometimes they come on if it's something really obvious. But, say I am going through the exercise of trying to find someone in the prime minster's office to speak on the Salman Rushdie affair. Everybody is wringing their hands. Nobody wants to do it. The Justice minister doesn't want to do it. The Immigration minister doesn't want to do it. The Minister of External Affairs doesn't want to do it because it wasn't on his agenda. There is a very odd approach to this kind of thing.

If this were the States, there's no question I could get someone on. Obviously there were days when George Shultz didn't want to go on and discuss the Iran-contra affair. But generally, if you want to discuss defence policy, or negotiations in the Middle East, the players are there. Does David Brinkley or *Meet the Press* have a problem getting the key cabinet minister every week? Absolutely not. They are lined up at the door. They believe it is their job to get their message out. And it's the press's job to critique those views or ask questions. But they believe the public has the right to know and, one must not be naive, they want an opportunity to put their own spin on it.

When Washington-based CBC *producer* **Marc Allard**
*travelled to China with Pierre Trudeau, Allard caught an
up-close glimpse of a man who would later become one of the
world's most reviled leaders. Back then, however, Deng
Xiaoping seemed like a harmless old grandmother.*

When I was in Beijing with Trudeau, I met Deng Xiaoping. I
sat fascinated watching this little old man, the leader of this
great country, sitting in a great old armchair from the fifties
with a spittoon next to him. He's sitting next to Trudeau just
letting off these big huge spitballs into a pan. And I mean, they
made noise! The sight of that was only topped by the roasted
dog for dinner.

Front Page Challenge producer **Lorraine Thomson**
remembers a not-so-magnanimous Maggie Trudeau.

I remember standing beside Prime Minister Trudeau — calm,
cool Trudeau — when he was a guest on our show. His knees
were shaking. His pant legs were literally vibrating, he was so
nervous. When we have a prime minister on — and we've had
them all except Mulroney — they get the whole half-hour
with no commercial interruptions.

Margaret was waiting for Trudeau in our green room. After
he finished on air, Margaret didn't say anything about how
he'd done. She just said: "The baby needs to be changed."
And off he went to do it.

*The most intriguing characters met on the job may not be
famous, just outlandish.* The Journal *soundman* **Alister Bell**
recalls a bizarre birthday spent with the Iraqi army.

In 1984, I was sent to cover the Iraqi side of the war with Iran.
We were taken by helicopter to the frontlines and spent the
night in the barracks with the artillery battalion. The plan was
to head out very early the next morning to film the fearless
Iraqi soldiers shelling Iranian territory. At 6:00 a.m. we
headed off in a truck to the artillery positions. I looked at the
date on my watch and noticed it was my birthday. Everybody
got quite excited at the news and shook my hand. Thank God
they didn't want to kiss me — I guess they were happy
enough just kissing each other constantly.

Eventually we arrived at the spot where the Howitzers were
positioned. The plan seemed to be to line these guns up on an
Iranian village twenty-five kilometres away, shell it, and, presumably, kill everybody living there — or, at the very least,
scare the hell out of them.

We filmed the huge guns being loaded with shells and the
charge to send them on their way. At this point, the commander came over to me. "I hear it's your birthday. I would
like you to have the honour of firing the gun." I was completely shocked. "No, no, I couldn't," I said. "Oh, you must,"
he insisted. "It's a present. It's really easy, and it's all ready to
fire."

I tried to imagine my next postcard home: Dear Mum, have
just shelled an Iranian village, must have breakfast now. Or, a

headline in the *Baghdad Bugle*: CBC soundman lands direct hit on Iranian village, kills thousands, mainly children. Eventually, I persuaded the commander that it would be best if one of his boys did the deed and I just watched. He was extremely disappointed that I had turned down the honour of killing Iranians.

In 1988, before Sting and David Suzuki made it fashionable,
Journal *producer* **Harry Phillips** *travelled to Brazil to do a
story about the destruction of the Amazon rain forest. It
seemed a straightforward assignment until Phillips discovered
that the Indian tribe he and his crew were to visit had a
habit of skewering visitors.*

Eight years before our visit, the Kayapo of Aukre village, deep
in the Amazon jungle, had massacred the last sizeable group of
white folks to visit their territory. After that, the Brazilian
government had declared Indian land out of bounds to non-
Indians. That was enough for our Portuguese-English translator to change his mind about the thrill of coming with us.
Stuck in a town on the edge of the rain forest, we had to find
another translator fast. Along came Paulo, the local English
teacher. Paulo's English was atrocious but, we were desperate. Twenty-four hours later, we were all in Aukre, airlifted
one hundred kilometres deep into the forest, unloading our
equipment amid a throng of naked Kayapo armed with spears.

In attempting to translate the initial pleasantries, Paulo
somehow offended the Kayapo chief. I hoped the chief would
notice the cardboard boxes being unloaded from the plane.
They contained gifts for his people, our only tangible as-
surance of safety. Then it occurred to me that one of the gift
boxes contained forty hunting knives.

An hour later, our link with the outside world was severed.
The plane with the newly fired Paulo on board was gone. An
English-speaking Brazilian woman who happened to be visit-

ing the village with her American husband became translator number three. Zilda established that the only person who spoke even a little Portuguese was the chief, who had disappeared. Zilda spoke no Kayapo. We handed out the gifts. The sun was going down, and *The Journal* was huddled in four hammocks inside a mud hut at the edge of the village. The Kayapo were now armed with spears and sharp, new hunting knives.

A family of Kayapo suddenly entered our hut and sat down, content, it seemed, just to watch us. I gave whistles to the children, Terry Fox shoelaces to Mom, and pictures of George Bell, Roger Clemens, Dave Winfield, and a San Diego Padre to Dad. They were all pleased except Dad, who pointed his new hunting knife at my battery-powered table lamp. I refused *very gently*. He took his family and left, only to be replaced by another family, whom we similarly entertained. They were replaced by another and another until, we guessed, most of the village had passed through our hut and cleaned out our gifts. By now it was midnight, under a full moon, and the village echoed with the shrill sounds of about two dozen tiny plastic whistles. The whistles were such a great hit that I began to worry about a kid swallowing one by accident and choking to death. What would they do to me? It was enough to keep me awake all night.

The next morning virtually all the children in the village were wearing old shoes with new Terry Fox shoelaces. Whistles and macaws were engaged in a competitive ruckus. We taped the village and the Indians going about their business, but something was definitely amiss. The acting chief seemed to have lost his congenial disposition. He turned even cooler when we made it understood that our airplane would pick us up later that day.

Back in Canada, I discovered that we had committed two very serious social errors. First, we were obliged to visit the huts of every family that paid a visit to our hut. Second, when one is invited to stay in Aukre, one does not leave until invited to do so by the chief. The men of the village had angrily converged on the chief, waving their spears — and our knives — demanding to know why they had been slighted. Apparently they had been out hunting monkeys when we left, or they would have confronted us instead. About the same time, I heard a report about a British documentary crew who had left some of their team in a Kayapo village while they went out for supplies. When they returned after a few days, the village and crew were gone, never to be heard from again.

The Journal's sports specialist, **Tom Alderman,** *got an intimate glimpse into the inner-life of the Scottish soccer fan when he chose to travel to the 1984 World Cup Games in Spain aboard a rickety double-decker bus.*

They would not have been my chosen bedfellows. Nevertheless, to tell the World Cup story from the point of view of the fan, we had chosen to follow this motley crew from their home in Maybole in County Ayr, south through England and France and on to Spain to cheer for their countrymen. I would journey with them from Maybole to southern France — three days and three nights in that bus — the better to get to know them. We would be joined in Bordeaux by my producer, cameraman, and soundman, at which time we would begin shooting the documentary.

I arrived in Maybole the night before we were to leave. I was immediately whisked to the Gluepot, the soccer fans' local — a grimy, dark, miserable pub with a dirt floor, where martinis are not served. In the gloom, staunch members of the drinking class sat grim-faced along the wall, downing Scotch after Scotch till they pitched headfirst into the muck of the dirt floor.

Next morning, to a smattering of cheers from the townspeople, we set off in the double-decker, most of the dirty dozen still trying to shake off the effects of the night before. The most sober of the lot was left to drive. He had not brought a map. *No one* had brought a map. But they didn't need one, they reasoned. They were just going south.

We got through Scotland all right. England wasn't bad. We

even got across the English Channel reasonably well. But France got sticky. Table manners had broken down by now. The bus toilet had also broken down, necessitating the use of a hole punched in the floor. The sleeping quarters on the upper deck had degenerated into a surreal madhouse of snoring, groaning, flatulating bodies. We also didn't know where we were going. None of them could — or would — speak a word of French to ask directions. We took a lot of wrong turns.

One thing I *knew*, we should not drive through Paris. Around it, yes, but *not* through it. I warned the driver that, if he saw the word "Paris," he should drive in the opposite direction. Early Saturday evening, we found ourselves, naturally, in the heart of Paris — city of traffic jams, city of bridges. Double-decker buses do not fit under Parisian bridges. We got stuck. Hundreds of very annoyed drivers piled up behind. The gendarmes arrived, threatened to impound the bus, and ordered us out of town.

The driver wheeled south for about three blocks, and tried to go under *another* bridge. This time there seemed to be *thousands* of cars piled up behind us; drivers cursing, seething, ready to kill. The boys pranced among them in their kilts, offering beer. The gendarmes arrived again, happily a different crew. It took three hours to sort this one out. As the only one with some knowledge of French, I absorbed a tongue-lashing on behalf of the entire British Empire.

We rolled into Bordeaux just half a day late. I could see our camera crew as the double-decker wheezed into the parking lot of their luxury hotel. They were on the patio, contemplating the remnants of an excellent lunch and a bottle of the local product. The bus door opened and I flung myself out, an inmate wrongly imprisoned for a crime he didn't commit. I took an hour-long shower — the bathtub was caked with grime when I stepped out — and towelled off lazily.

I proceeded on through France and Spain, following the bus at a respectful distance — as with a rabid dog — in a rented car.

While covering the obscure, decade-long war between Chad and Libya, NBC's **Henry Champ** *discovered Africa's hottest nightclub act.*

It was a slow news period — because in the reality of the world, I can't imagine that anybody cares about Chadian affairs. But in 1983, Gaddafi and the French were fighting there, and somebody in New York says, "Jesus Christ! Gaddafi! We better get someone in there!" My name comes up and off I go. Chad is the worst place I've ever been.

We stayed at the Chadian Hotel — the only hotel — in N'Djamena. There was nothing there. We had to buy our own mattresses at the market, and put them on the balcony with mosquito netting over us because there were no beds in the rooms. The toilet was just a pipe coming out of the wall: there was no fixture on it. When I was peeing, I was never sure that the guy downstairs wasn't getting it in the face.

When the press arrived at this place — and it was the usual travelling-circus, gang-bang crowd — we were about one hundred strong. The French had an enormous crew of people since this was all part of their empire. The hotel was able to accommodate all of us because we just grabbed a piece of hallway, put up mosquito netting, and called it home. A plane from Gabon would fly our material in and out. There was no other contact with the office. No phone. No wire. No telex. No nothing. It was the poorest country in the entire world. Everyone was miserable.

One day we're driving along and we saw a little tattered sign that says the Chadian National Orchestra will be playing in a dairy barn that evening. A colleague and I went. The band had thirty people and twelve instruments. And could they wail! Wow! Chad being in the north, they had a mix of African, Egyptian and reggae music. I thought it was just the greatest thing I'd ever heard.

So, I go over to the leader and say, "Look, I want to hire you. How much would it cost to bring your boys over to the Chadian Hotel for a night?" They were very reluctant, but when I offered them four hundred dollars, we had a deal.

So, the next day I put up signs and passed the word — NBC presents . . . the Chadian National Orchestra. The deal was that everyone was invited, and, if they liked the music, as I was sure they would, they could chip in ten dollars to pay for it.

Now comes the band. They've brought two little girls for backup. And I'm really proud of myself. "Fellows, you are about to hear one of the great bands of all times . . ." All the press is there. The visiting Zairians have brought out all their top officers. All the diplomats are there. Everybody has heard about this thing. There's great excitement as I usher the band to the front.

The leader gets up, takes his place, and I feel great because I know they are all going to go nuts over this thing. And then out comes: "Feel-lings . . . Nothing more than feeel-lings . . . Feeeelings . . . of Loooove. . . ."

All eyes turn to me as though I am the dumbest jerk who ever lived. People are throwing bread rolls at me. I grab the band leader and a translator and say forcefully: "Okay, that was good. Now let's get back to that boogie stuff. Okay?"

The leader looks at me. He nods. And then: "I left my heart . . . in San Fransisco." Okay, that's it. I don't even let him finish. I grab him and the translator — to the profound laughter of the crowd. I tell the translator I want to ask the band a few questions.

He says, "Okay."

"How much did I agree to pay you?"

"Four hundred dollars."

"American?"

"American."

"Good. Now if you don't start playing what you played last night in the dairy barn, you are getting fuck all! Nothing! Game over! End of story!"

Well, they start up again and this time they wail. The whole place went nuts. The bread rolls stop flying and people stop leaving. Everybody's having a great time. At 10:00 p.m. I give the guys their four hundred dollars, but nobody wants to leave. They take up a collection, raise another four hundred, and keep them there till three in the morning. And could they play? Oh, could they play!

PERKS, PERILS, AND POINTERS

Job satisfaction among television correspondents is very high. At least, that's my conclusion after talking to so many of them. And, no doubt, there is a lot about the job to enjoy: prestige, regular travel, unconventional working hours, and getting close enough to eyeball the leading protagonists of our time.

But there *is* a price — dreary hotel rooms, inedible food, jet lag, language barriers and never having enough clean underwear. "There are times when you feel like you are travelling with a third-rate heavy metal band," sighs CBC *National* reporter Patrick Brown.

But the job makes up for the sacrifices with the greatest perk of all. As *The Journal*'s Tom Alderman puts it, "It's always much more fun travelling on someone else's money."

When he was working for the CBC *during the late sixties, cameraman* **Phil Pendry** *discovered that travelling in and out of the world's most fashionable wars impressed women a great deal. He capitalized on this discovery by packing along a beautiful young woman whenever he went abroad. He even figured how to do it at his company's expense. It is only because he is now retired that he is willing to share his know-how.*

When I was working for the CBC out of London, we would get paid thirty-five dollars a day to cover a story, plus fifty-cents a foot of film. I'd be sent to Geneva to cover peace conferences that went on for *hours.* In one month I earned two thousand dollars at a time when two thousand was worth a lot. But when I got back home, the CBC said: "Oh, we're terribly sorry, we've switched you from thirty-five dollars a story to seventy-five dollars a day, all inclusive." I felt ripped off but got my revenge.

I started saving up my "excess vouchers," which we would get to cover the cost of baggage and transportation. In no time, I built up a nice nest-egg of four to five thousand dollars. But I put them to good use — my excess baggage always took the form of a beautiful lady.

I could offer a woman a trip to the south of France — "Hey, you want to go the Cannes Film Festival?" And she'd say: "With you? Get lost." But Cyprus, Israel, any good war where the fighting is fierce, and a woman will always say: "Let's go!" I had found the perfect aphrodisiac for a woman — danger.

The night before we were all scheduled to fly down to the

Congo war, a bunch of us were sitting around in a bar, having a drink. In walked the most gorgeous girl. She was Patricia Fenn, the Craven "A" model in London. She was beautiful. Everybody had tried to date her but no one got anywhere. She sat down and I said to her: "Hey, how would you like to go down to the Congo?" She replied: "When are we leaving?" No one could believe it. My jaw dropped, too, but I certainly wasn't going to withdraw my offer. That's when I first learned women and danger mix well. Patricia eventually got into the business herself and married an NBC correspondent.

I took her to the Congo at the height of the trouble. We were met at the plane by CBC correspondent Michael Maclear. The look on his face when he saw us was unbelievable. "Who's this?" he asked.

"My soundperson."

"But CBC didn't hire her!"

"No, I did."

Once the correspondents figured out how it was that I always travelled with a beautiful woman by my side, they began demanding a portion of my excess baggage vouchers for themselves. Unfortunately the CBC figured it out, too. They wrote me a letter explaining I owed them eight thousand dollars for taking guests to Cyprus, the Congo, Israel, and Algeria.

I sent them a certified cheque for $325.63, explaining that this was the balance I owed after deducting what they owed me from Geneva. They transferred me to Japan after that.

Sleepless nights in strange surroundings are just part of the job and while, more often than not, correspondents find themselves holed up in the orange-and-brown splendour of some hotel-chain bedroom, occasionally they are forced to take up lodgings that fall on the other side of bizarre.
While following the Norman Bethune trail in the northern Chinese province of Hebei, CTV correspondent **Robert Hurst** *lucked into an unusual Oriental luxury.*

We were in a very remote part of the country and the hotel was really basic. Concrete floors, hard bed, no furniture at all, and just one bad telephone. They had a little dining room and the four of us ate around one small table. The staff really went out of their way. They were so happy to have some business and some customers. The hotel had been closed for ten years, but had reopened for the Canadian television crew coming in to spend a few days to do a documentary on the legendary Bethune. We were treated like visiting royalty.

At the end of our first evening there, before we retired, the manager warned us that they were having difficulty with the hot water and they hoped it would be satisfactory. We went in only to discover that it was wonderful hot water. In fact, it was scalding hot. The problem was that's *all* there was — out of both taps.

We would come off a day on the road, draw our bathwater at 6:00 p.m., go to dinner, and by 10:30 it would have cooled off. But the wonderful thing about it was that there was also hot water in the toilet. I don't know if you've ever sat on a steaming toilet — but it's really something. The condensation makes the seat very wet, it looks used. But when you've been out in the dusty, dirty Chinese countryside all day, and come home to sit on a steaming toilet with the scalding water vapours evaporating, you've felt heaven. We never asked them to change the cold water side; it was too wonderful.

Before he became an anchor, **Knowlton Nash** *spent many nights on the road as Washington correspondent for* CBC. *One of his less restful resting places was Detroit, Michigan —* Murder City.

First Class, it wasn't. Third, fourth, or fifth class, it wasn't. It had a category all its own. When I reached the American Plaza Hotel in Detroit for the Republican Convention, which started Ronald Reagan on his way to the White House, I was back in the shambles of the race riots that I'd covered in Detroit thirteen years before. To say the hotel was rundown would be flattering. It seemed to be falling down — with a wobbly card table as a reception desk, broken glass scattered about the floor, and broken windows here and there. Outside, there were loitering individuals you'd be leery of meeting in bright sunlight.

A large-stomached gentleman by the name of Mr. Eddy and his very large German shepherd dog snarled their greetings.

"Whattaya want?" Mr. Eddy inquired.

As my colleagues and I explained, we were from the CBC and were covering the Republican Convention and had reservations. Mr. Eddy, who appeared to be both the manager and sole employee of the hotel, opened a drawer, pushed aside a revolver, and pulled out a long, dirty crumpled sheet of paper.

"Oh, yeah!" he said, swishing his unlit but well-chewed cigar to the other side of his mouth. "It's room 408 for Nash."

I picked up my bags and walked uneasily into a decrepit elevator. To my surprise, it moved, albeit creakily and jerkily.

When I got to room 408, I found I didn't need a key since the door was already broken and unlockable. The room was straight out of a lost weekend in the Bowery: a narrow, hard bed, a sheet, a horse blanket, a paint-peeled dresser, a string dangling down from an overhead light bulb, and a toilet that, when it flushed, let out a banshee howl of protest. There was a TV set that probably once worked, and a window, which of course, didn't open, overlooking the garbage-strewn, pot-holed street below.

Coming from the convention hall every night, it was hard to persuade cab drivers to go into the area. "Are you crazy?" the first one I picked shouted at me as he drove off. "I wouldn't go up there for anything. I value my life." When questioned about the quality of the accommodations and the safety of the hotel, Mr. Eddy commented archly, "We ain't had nobody raped or any cars stolen for a week."

After the convention was over and we had departed our First Class hotel, I bought my colleagues T-shirts emblazoned with I SURVIVED THE AMERICAN PLAZA. It was all part of the allegedly glamorous life of a foreign correspondent.

CBC correspondent **Claude Adams** *found what may be cheapest lodging in the known universe, in Nicaragua.*

For the equivalent of about twenty cents, the Pension Vargas in San Rafael, Nicaragua, will offer you a stall with a cot and blanket for the night. It is the ultimate in no-frills accommodation: no reading light, no table, no chair; nothing but a cot and threadbare blanket in an eight-by-four foot room, and a rooster to wake you up a half-hour before dawn. Guests should button shirt cuffs and tuck pant cuffs into socks to keep out roaches and biting insects. I was tired enough to sleep through virtually anything. Except for one thing — the room next to mine was occupied by a young honeymooning couple spending their wedding night, we learned later, away from her parents' home. They would be returning the next morning, but, meanwhile, a noisy night of love in stall number six of the Pension Vargas.

Senora Vargas doesn't give receipts, so this jewel of an inn has never appeared on an expense account.

*On the road, journalists are often required to accept the
hospitality of strange, but potentially useful people. If, for
example, an Inuit source can butcher seal and caribou and
find it especially tempting while it's still steaming, the
journalist tucks in. He may not need the meal but he needs
his meal-ticket. Nonetheless, when a foreign correspondent
has to choose between hunger or downing the local delicacy
of chicken-eyeball paste, the job can lose some of its appeal.*
NBC's **Henry Champ** *stresses the importance of being polite.*

It doesn't matter if you are doing a story on Winnipeg or
Wamba; if you want to know what's going on, you must
create a bond by breaking bread with your subject, no matter
what it is that he is serving. People won't tell you anything
unless they like you. It only takes a minute for your subject to
decide — "Oh well, forget about this guy in the Burberry
coat, he's not interested in what we're talking about."

If you are in Northern China, and somebody says: "Hey,
Mr. Champ, we have a local delicacy here. It's dog," what are
you going to do? You're going to eat it. They're proud of it. It's
a matter of respect. Maybe they killed the best dog in the yard
for you.

Dog tastes a bit like veal. Since they're raised for food
consumption, they're kept in cages, like chickens. I've eaten
it a number of times, but I wouldn't call myself a dog-meat
lover.

The Chinese also eat live snake. The waiter comes to your
table with seven of them wrapped around his arm and asks
which one you'd like. They take your choice, put it through a

hole in the table, reach underneath . . . and off with it's head, it's skinned. While it is still quivering, they chop it up and away you go. I had to eat it. I was with some people I needed to impress. Eating the snake was *de rigueur*, but I don't believe I ate the whole thing.

In Afghanistan, dinner was often made by slaughtering goats, skinning them, and throwing them into boiling water, with all the fat congealing on the top. It was awful. You had to chew a small piece sixteen thousand times to get it down. But it was fresh. And the water was hot, so I figured it was safe. They always made a bread, and when we were near a village, the mujahideen supporters would give us sugar, cucumbers, and tomatoes. But when there were no villages, we had to make do with goat.

Much-travelled W5 *producer* **Malcolm Fox** *cautions against baluk in the Philippines and salads in Egypt.*

In Gabon they make a paste out of the eyeball of chickens and consider it a great specialty. In the Philippines, covering the elections, we discovered a related delicacy called baluk. It's a fertilized chicken egg developed to the point where the chicken inside is totally formed, except the tissue is still soft. So, you have a chicken inside an egg — with a perfect bone structure, a beak, feathers, but no hard tissue. They boil them and kids sell them from the backs of their bikes in the streets and in the bars.

What they do is cut the top of the egg off, and this perfectly formed chicken is sitting there. Then they knock it back, chew it up, and wash it down with beer. I wouldn't eat it, but the reporter and cameraman did. They said it tasted, as you'd imagine, like a cross between a hard-boiled egg and a chicken.

A few years earlier, in Cairo, we stayed with the Canadian Armed Forces in a UN camp on the outskirts of the city. They put us up in the space that they had available — a tent, used as a chapel on Sundays. It was a tent like all the others except for a rough wooden altar and a cross. They put in a couple of camp cots for us.

On the second day, I came down with a really bad case of what they call "Gypo-Gut." I'd made the stupid mistake of eating a salad, and when I woke up the next morning I thought I was going to die. I was laid out on my cot in this tent. The sun would shine through the flaps and cast the shadow of a cross across my chest. During the day the temperature inside was at least 130 degrees. People would bring me warm water to drink. I couldn't eat and knew I just had to wait it out.

By day two, when I was very dehydrated, somebody went over to the PX to get me a can of Orange Crush. It was ice cold, unlike everything else I had to drink. I drank as much of it as I could, but that turned out to be only a couple of sips. Exhausted, I put the can back on the ground and fell asleep.

I slept for about two hours, and when I woke, I reached down and picked up the can of Orange Crush, which was now like hot tea. But I was so thirsty, I didn't care. I put the can up to my lips and started drinking. I drank two or three gulps when I noticed that the whole can was black. And my arm was black. And my chest was turning black. And my face. The can of Orange Crush had turned into a mass of ants. Tiny ants. They were crawling in my mouth and on my face. I spit out the soda and rolled over. If I'd had a gun I would have blown my head off.

The Journal *correspondent* **Bruce Garvey,** *who claims that in Vietnam he was served deep-fried swallows thrown live into boiling fat, describes another memorable meal.*

One time, in Cameroon, we were on our way to the Yaounde, up-country from the sweatbox humidity of Douala, cleverly located by the French on a coastal swamp designed for disease and early death. One day out of Douala, we pulled up to our hotel, which stood on the banks of a muddy yellow creek, where a waterlogged flat raft served as a ferry. The beds were as worn and filthy as the corrugated iron roof; the kitchen we dared not imagine. We had no little trepidation about the evening meal.

It was Jean-Guy Nault who ordered, after earnest conversation in French out of which I only picked up the word "porc-épic." The waiter bustled off and Guy told me: "Look, it was boiled chicken and rice or the specialty of the day, which was fresh, and that's what we're having."

"What is it?" I ventured.

"Porcupine," Jean-Guy said, smiling "and they know it's fresh because they scraped it off the road this morning. A truck hit it."

Actually, it wasn't bad.

In the Falkland Islands, **Hana Gartner** *was served the local speciality every day, three times a day.*

I became sheep-phobic after our visit to the Falkland Islands. We were staying at a place called the Upland Goose, run by a woman named Mrs. King. The inn was like one of those nineteenth-century seashore inns they make series about on Thames Television. The toilets were down the hall, an old threadbare chenille spread over the bed, you heard people take a bath next door — that kind of thing. The place was packed full of reporters, especially BBC people, because her inn was the only place to stay on the island.

Mrs. King almost killed us. She was the most sour, humourless lady I have ever met. And her cooking! Everything Mrs. King cooked tasted like sheep. It's understandable since the only other thing on the island is peat moss. We're not talking New Zealand spring lamb — sheep! I think they fed the chickens sheep bones because even the eggs tasted like it. One night we had a bet on. What was it? Was it chicken? Was it sheep? It turned out to be fish! Fish fried in sheep dip. To this day, I cannot smell sheep. I will not eat sheep. I am totally sheep-phobic.

Another unforgettable series of meals was had with the Ohanuit, the People of the Deer, in the Arctic. These people were the last tribe to wander around the interior of the Arctic. Until the 1950s, they thought they were the only people on earth.

The Ohanuit were not seal hunters. And when the caribou migration patterns changed, they started to starve. The

127

federal government, in the prevailing wisdom of the 1950s, put them in a settlement. Thirty years later, the elders wanted to make a return visit to their ancestral homeland before they all died out, to briefly recapture the way they had lived. A real goosebumps-on-your-kneecaps story — I loved it.

We flew in with thirty Inuit elders, most of whom did not speak English. The plane was going to come back for us in seven days, with luck, if the weather was good. The Inuit were going to stay for two weeks.

When we arrived to set up camp, there was . . . nothing! Nothing! It was tundra. I fail to grasp the warm feelings people have for some locations. For these people, this was home. For Hana this was major torture. I have taken trips that were arduous, but I thought I was going to die in the Arctic.

Of course, I was well-appointed in my Eddie Bauer Yuppie Arctic-wear. After all, I had to appear on camera, though by the end, my hat pulled over my ears, I looked a pathetic mess.

Once we were set up, it was time to go hunting. Why else did the elders want to come home! Their dream, their life, is caribou. They knew how to live on it and use every part of it. So, we had to go hunting. Hunting! I get queasy in the meat section at Dominion. My first reaction was to weep because these incredible, beautiful animals who hadn't been hunted in ages, practically stood still in their tracks, staring at you with these big brown eyes. They would crash down. It was very hard on me.

They butchered and eviscerated the caribou in about ten minutes, then packed up to walk back to camp. Since I was part of this, I had to help. They weren't going to carry me on a litter. Immediately my new Eddie Bauer outfit was christened with a knapsack of seeping viscera bleeding down my back. When we arrived at the camp, I thought to myself — I'll rest while they prepare this stuff. Prepare? No! They got out these special knives, whacked off a chunk of caribou, the steam rising off the animal, and offered me the first taste — raw.

At this point, I figured there was no way I was going to be able to ingratiate myself with these people. I explained through interpreters that if I ate this raw piece of meat, I would die. Please don't feel insulted. They were very nice and smiled and said they understood. They ate every part of this animal, including a macaroni substance out of the hooves. They sucked the marrow out of the bones. They'd explain that the reason I was freezing to death was because I was not eating caribou, which gives you insulation. I was living on soda crackers and tea. The only thing I did eat was the tuna. I told myself it was sushi. It was missing the green mustard but otherwise I had no problem with it.

Like Gartner, W5 host **Jim Reed** *went to the Arctic to discover that there is indeed such a thing as Canadian cuisine.*

Gordon Henderson and I went to Cape Dorset in 1979 with Kiawak — a great Inuit sculptor. He took us in his canoe across the Arctic Ocean to his summer home, where he collects the bones, stones, and skeletons he uses to make his sculptures.

As we were zipping along in his canoe — it was a huge thing with an outboard motor — I hear the crack of a gun going off right by my head. He'd shot a seal.

We steer over to it, drag it into the boat beside me, and continue on our way. On shore, forty-five minutes later, we drag the seal from the boat. This becomes the number-one priority. Nothing else matters. They take it over to a rock, the knives are out, they're pulling out the blubber and eating it right there.

Kiawak turns to me and asks, "What do you want?"

So I say: "What's good?"

He says, "Liver is very good."

"Okay I'll take some liver."

With hands covered in blood, he grabs a piece of the liver and, as I reach out to take it, he says, "Oh, no. Open your mouth." So I did, and he drops this piece of liver in. It was still warm. Actually it tasted quite good, like almonds.

*One definite perk of a life spent on the road is the opportunity
to shop for exotic foreign goods. The voyages of* CBC *anchor*
Peter Mansbridge *have netted him some unusual souvenirs.*

It was May 1976, and I was in China, covering Premier Allan
Blakeney's attempt to sell Saskatchewan potash to the Chinese. It was a difficult trip for Blakeney because China was in
the midst of turmoil. Chairman Mao was in his last days, and
there was a tremendous struggle underway between forces of
the left and right. As a result, Blakeney kept being shuffled off
on tours: the Great Wall, the Forbidden City, the model farm
commune at Da Chai, and the Herbal Medicine Clinic in
Shanghai.

As one of only two journalists covering this story, I obviously had to travel along on all the tours. While all were
fascinating, I took a strong personal interest in the Herbal
Clinic. The people there claimed they had a cure for literally
everything. Well, I was in the early days of realizing that I was
losing my hair, and, if they had cures, I was in the market.

The clinic officials listened intently as I outlined the problem, and when the translation was completed, there were a
few snickers but also a solution. They told me all Chinese
drugstores had the herbal remedy for this, and then scribbled
out a prescription in Chinese. I couldn't get out of there fast
enough to get the prescription filled.

In those days, travel in China was very limited, but I did
manage to convince my guide-interpreter-driver-spy that this
was an issue that struck to the heart of better Chinese-Canadian relations. He agreed we'd find a drugstore. And we

did, along the Bund ... the drive along the waterfront in downtown Shanghai. The pharmacy was located in a grand old British bank building, which had been converted in the post-1949 period into a people's department store. A crowd of a couple hundred Chinese were gathered as this strange, tall Caucasian stood at the counter with a prescription. It took a while, but finally through translation the druggist had good news — they had the pills required. I asked how many bottles did they have? The answer came back — twenty-four. I asked to buy them all. I figured I could make a fortune out of this. For about fifty Canadian dollars, the deal was made.

Two weeks later, I was back in Canada with the goods and the growing conviction that my hair problem was about to be solved. The instructions called for me to take fifteen pills a day for seven days, and repeat every month. That was a lot of pills, so I decided I'd better have them analysed just to make sure. The city medical health officer in Regina at the time was a Chinese Canadian who had emigrated from China post-1949. He said he'd take a look. Two days later he called back, and I''ll never forget the conversation:

"Mr. Mansbridge," said the doctor.

"Yes, that's me."

"I've analysed the pills you brought back."

"Yes," I said, with anticipation.

"Sorry, but they will do nothing for your hair."

"What!" I said. "They promised me this was the real cure."

"Well, Mr. Mansbridge, these are very old pills from China. In fact, I remember them well, and they will do nothing for your hair."

"I can't believe this," I said, "they promised!"

"Well, Mr. Mansbridge, I"'m sorry but these don't have anything to do with hair."

"So, what are they for?" I asked.

"Well, as I said, I remember these pills when I was in China. And they are for another age-old problem."

There was a short pause and then the answer — "Aphrodisiacs."

CBC *reporter* **Dan Bjarnason** *had no more luck shopping in Poland than a Warsaw housewife.*

In December 1980, covering the birth of Solidarity, I tried to do some late shopping for Christmas gifts in a land that has nothing to sell. I asked my sympathetic "keeper":

"I need some help here looking for presents. What is Poland famous for? What can I take back home as a gift that would make a nice memory?"

"Nothing."

"Come on. There must be something. I'm not after anything elaborate. Something typically Polish. Something that will remind me of this place."

"No. Truly. Nothing. There is nothing here at all."

"Come now. How about some Polish ham? I could get it packed for shipment. All the world knows of Poland's famous hams."

"Mister. You want Polish ham? Go to London and shop at Harrod's. There is no Polish ham in Poland."

Journal soundman **Alister Bell** *remarks on the emotional wear and tear wrought by rapid travel between the serenity of home and some convincing simulations of hell-on-earth.*

I went to Bhopal, India, with Ann Medina. Bhopal is where it really came home to me what we do. You can be sitting in downtown Toronto, and the Union Carbide tank leaks lethal gas. Within thirty-six hours you're in Bhopal. You've left your comfortable little home on the Scarborough bluffs and you're seeing one of the world's great disasters with your own eyes. You're watching people die in front of you. Dropping dead. You film it all. It's not like you're there for UNICEF. You have a documentary to do. You've got editors in Toronto saying get us this and get us that. You work your ass off for two days and then get back on a 747 jet to Toronto.

Within ten days, you've been back and forth to India and witnessed the deaths of thousands of people. And, yet, when you return home, you continue to attend all the pre-Christmas eggnog parties and talk to your neighbours about the new sewage system. It's jarring on the system.

Anyone considering a career in foreign reporting might wish to take note of the following tricks of the trade, none of which is taught in journalism school.

1. PACK LOTS OF U.S. CAPITALIST PRODUCTS ON TRIPS TO CUBA
CBC *reporter* Dan Bjarnason

When travelling in Iron Curtain countries, it is wise to bring money substitutes. In Cuba, for example, North American cigarettes, chewing gum, and chocolate bars are sure winners. Anything denim is worth its weight in rum, but it's not practical to go through Havana customs with a suitcase full of blue jeans. Take along as much lipstick, rouge, nylons, finger-nail polish, or women's undergarments as you feel you can without blushing. Most such goods Cuban women get are from Russia. They're junk and no one wants them. Cosmetics from the People's Beautification Collective and Tractor Factory in Magnitogorsk have the consistency of Crisco. You can offer your cosmetics to Cubans you want to impress or influence without technically offering a bribe, which in Cuba is big trouble. The magic of offering cosmetics and, the like to your "keepers" and the officials you must deal with, and, likely as not, they will be males, is that the gifts are for their wives and/or girlfriends. The man will instantly realize what a gold mine he has here and, from this point on, will die for you.

2. BRING GIFTS FOR GUERRILLAS
CBC *correspondent* **Claude Adams**

Working in Nicaragua and El Salvador, we learned an important lesson from the old network hands. When you rent a car,
never have it washed or cleaned. A perpetual layer of dust and
grime is essential because it makes it easier to spot any tamper-
ing with the vehicle, i.e., the placing of a bomb. Also, keep
enormous quantities of American cigarettes and soft drinks in
the trunk as gifts. This got me out of a sticky spot in the
jungles of northern Nicaragua. A Sandinista sergeant took a
fancy to my shiny new Swiss army knife, and said he wanted
it. His had rusted beyond repair, and he noted that mine had
the magnifying glass, scissors, fish scaler, three screwdriver
heads, corkscrew, and hacksaw: everything he needed in the
field. I politely said I preferred to keep it, but he became more
and more insistent, and even menacing. He offered me his
spare boots as barter. When I turned that down, he snarled
and made a move to grab the knife from my waist. His squad
was watching with great interest the baiting of a gringo visitor.
Finally, I gave him three cartons of Marlboros and half a
dozen Cokes, and that distracted him enough for us to make
our getaway.

3. BUY BULLET PROOF VESTS . . . ONLY IN SHADES OF BLUE
CTV *reporter* **Craig Oliver**

A vest costs about six hundred dollars. They are made of DuPont Kevlar. It is a bonded, space-age material used in airplanes and boats, nearly indestructible, and light for its size. They weigh about six pounds each. They also make bullet-resistant safari jackets, raincoats, and, even, undershirts. Colours vary, but the most appropriate is not the fashionable military dun shade. Tan and brown can too easily make you look like a combatant. Robin's egg blue is the most healthy colour.

To be sure that you won't have a customs problem, it is often useful to check with the authorities before carrying them in with you. In many Central American nations, such as El Salvador, a police permit is required. They want to be sure the vests leave with you and do not fall into the hands of guerrillas or contras.

Once, near San Salvador, a patrol of armed revolutionaries appeared out of the underbrush. They forced our vehicle over, put us up against the wall for body searches, then required us to "volunteer" our watches, cash, and our whole supply of cold beer. They left wearing spanking new armoured vests — *por la revolución!*

Some people fear that wearing a vest can invite hostility. There is a danger it may give the wearer a false sense of security and encourage the taking of unnecessary risks. But anyone who is going someplace where there might be shooting should not depend on his vest for protection. Depend on good judgement. Best of all, use the technique I employ increasingly these days — don't go!

4. REMEMBER TO CHECK YOUR BATTERIES
CBC *reporter* **Terry Milewski**

When transmitting material from the Third World, keep a close eye on the "professional" help. I remember trying to do a television satellite-feed out of Damascus, and being utterly frustrated because our tape machine just wouldn't work. Our Syrian "technician" had unplugged the machinery necessary for us to make our very expensive satellite-feed to Toronto — to boil the water for his tea.

5. DON'T TAKE DRUGS
CTV *anchor* **Lloyd Robertson**

It was budget day in Canada, and I had a terrible earache. On my way to the airport for my flight from Toronto to Ottawa for the budget speech TV broadcast, I stopped off at a drugstore and casually purchased a benign-looking brand of eardrops that were recommended to ease my problem. When I arrived in the capital, I placed a few drops in my ear and headed for Parliament Hill in the certain knowledge that relief would soon come. What a shock! In about an hour the area around my left ear was a swollen mass. My cheek was starting to swell and the whole thing was getting itchy. Realizing I was probably suffering an allergic reaction to the eardrops, I tried to call a doctor but had no luck. One hour to airtime. The make-up person did her best, but as the broadcast began I still had to appear on national television with a badly swollen face. The director kept the cameras far away from me most of the evening and the only reaction I had came from some colleagues in the Toronto newsroom who said I should know better than to get so hung over the night before a big show. Need I say more? Always read the labels on anything you're buying from the shelf anywhere in the world, including here at home.

6. WORK WITH A GOOD TRANSLATOR
CTV *cameraman* Jim Mercer

On one European trip, we had an effervescent young female producer who kept exclaiming "*Ja som hotovy*" whenever things were going well. At last, our polite Czechoslovakian guide could not contain his curiosity any longer. He blurted out: "Why do you keep repeating that silly phrase?"

"That's not silly at all," she replied. "My boyfriend is Czechoslovakian, and he says it all the time. It simply means, 'I am happy.' "

"I hate to disillusion you," he said, "but what he is really saying is, 'I am finished.' "

7. WEAR A WEDDING RING
CBC *reporter* Ann Medina

Always wear a wedding ring in the Middle East. It saves all kinds of trouble. It's also best to lie about having children. All women must have children, and it's too hard explaining to them why one might not.

8. BRING ENOUGH SOCKS
CTV *reporter* **Alan Edmonds**

I knew the romance of being a globetrotter had worn off when, having done one jet hijack and dropped in on two of those eternal Middle East wars, I was sent on to Delhi by a foreign editor who'd never been farther than Ottawa and had only a small-scale map. I'd never been to India, but when I got there I wasn't interested in how to find the Taj Mahal or Gandhi's birthplace. I'd been moving around too much too fast to get laundry done, and at night my socks stood up in the corner of whatever hotel room I could find. So, my priority on landing at New Delhi was to find the bazaar and a sock shop. They didn't have any size twelves, so I bought tens, cut off the toes, and suffered agony for the next two weeks, looking for an alleged Chinese incursion of India's mountain borders.

9. GO NATIVE
NBC *reporter* Henry Champ

In Afghanistan, I dressed in the tribal gear. You had to. At six foot three inches and *my* weight, no one was going to mistake me for an Afghan. I did it to fool the Soviets who monitored the territory from hilltop forts and observation points. The idea was to dress up the foreigner so that, at least through binoculars, he looked authentic.

If the Soviets thought we looked like Americans, they would have killed us. They would have assumed we were mischief-makers: CIA, or whatever. They would have called a helicopter and zapped us. Usually if you can identify yourself as a journalist, you're okay. But when you're travelling with the mujahideen, you can't walk around with a billboard reading NBC!

There was a case in Lebanon where a CBS crew was filming on a hillside. The Americans mistook CBS's camera for an RPG [rocket-propelled grenade], and killed them. So long as you can identify yourself as a journalist, you can generally do whatever you want, but sometimes that's hard to do.

So, I wore the long robe and the loose pyjama pants. I could roll my own turban — seven yards of silk. It would take an Afghan a microsecond to know you've got one of the boys down here, but I looked good from a distance.

In a war zone, you never carry a weapon, under any circumstances. Never. If you are captured and are in possession of a weapon, it's hard to convince people that you are a noncombatant.

143

COVERING THE WARS

Although most rational people go to great lengths to avoid danger, foreign correspondents appear to embrace it with delight.

It's only appearance. Actually, most foreign correspondents deny that they are violence-junkies. They insist that they do not enjoy the sight of blood or the whine of flying bullets. I believe them. But let's be frank: without it, TV journalists would have to spend a lot more time covering agricultural trade fairs. And we'd have to watch.

The challenge for a reporter is to get close enough to danger to seem authoritative but not so close as to need surgery. The test is knowing the difference between Pulitzer Prize proximity and imminent extinction. "I can't report the news if I'm dead" is the refrain of journalists explaining why they prefer to hang back when the shells start flying.

Is foreign reporting as dangerous as it looks? Maybe not. But when I asked some veterans to talk about it, they made it sound harrowing.

In an eight-year period as a foreign correspondent, **Brian Stewart** *has witnessed half a dozen wars and four famines, and has learned to live with fear.*

The days of reporters' wild booze-swilling forays through foreign conflicts belong to a fast-receding past. There are simply too many risks to the system. In and out of refugee camps, combat hospitals, and famine zones — you're bombarded with diseases. Meningitis in this ward, cholera in that; here tuberculosis, there diphtheria. Malaria, always a danger, can wreck a career; tetanus, from a simple cut, can ruin a $190,000 trip. Since AIDS, we carry special equipment to avoid local transfusions, enough to keep us going until we can be medivacked to safety.

One thing that's changed in the eighties — the risk of being injured in the field is now far greater, and, in areas where we work, medical services are deteriorating dramatically. Recently, in southern Sudan, I was in a besieged town where the local hospital had ceased to function. There were no drugs and no anesthetics. Amputations were done with the patient wide awake, as in the American Civil War. It was not a place one wanted to step on a land-mine or take a bullet.

News organizations must be the only institutions in the world that happily send people into war zones without so much as a minute's first-aid training. No self-respecting relief organization or diplomatic mission would send personnel into high-risk areas without survival training. The CBC now sends in teams who are experienced and well equipped with first-aid supplies. But I've rarely come across television or

147

print people in the field who've even taken a St. John Ambulance course, or would have a clue what to do for a bullet wound or shock. I've seen television crews collapse because they'd never been taught how to avoid dehydration. And, when we first start out, we all get needlessly sick because we've never learned how to handle food properly.

If I was in charge of a news organization, I'd make at least a first-aid course mandatory for anyone going into a foreign crisis spot. I'd make sure it included a survivor's guide to tropical diseases.

This generation of reporters and crews — unlike those in the late 1950s and 1960s — goes to war zones knowing remarkably little about war. They've usually had no military training, and often have never heard a shot fired in anger. They can't tell "incoming" from "outgoing" artillery fire, have no idea how to look for land-mines, and couldn't tell a battalion from a division if it marched over them. Most worrying — they seem to have only a rough idea of the destructive power of modern weapons. The result is that not only is our coverage of war frequently inadequate and confused, but the risks taken are preposterous.

In war zones, one comes quickly to understand the different states of tension and fear. One learns the remarkable idiosyncrasies of the nervous system, and you grow used to long periods of extraordinary alertness.

Tension in Beirut was constant and some of us showed signs of becoming addicted to the excitement. Getting through each day was a challenge, and so each day became a personal mountain. When we left, we joked about the "Beirut twitch," which left us jumpy and explosively irritable for weeks afterwards. Once back in England, I complained to my dentist that my jaw seemed to ache a lot. He said it was from grinding my teeth while I slept.

Fear, of course, is different from mere tension. True, big-league, all-star-game fear that leaves one nearly paralysed. Fear erupts within you in so many ways. You're driving down a street that should be full of traffic but is unaccountably empty. Everyone in the car tenses. You grip the door handle and silently will the driver to do something brilliant. Conversation stops. Someone mutters: "I don't like the look of this," but no one answers. You wonder if the others can smell your fear, and know for sure they'll hear it in your voice if you speak. You count the seconds . . . something to do.

Real war is remarkably and shockingly different from the movie concept of combat. It's so damn chaotic! And noisy! In 1983 I spent several days around the U.S. Marine base while it was being heavily shelled by Druze militia. Lying in a ditch once, while mortars crashed around us, I was fascinated how violent it all seemed, and kept thinking of the phoney shell-fire sounds of films like *Sands of Iwo Jima*. Mortars actually went BAAANNNNGGGGG with a brutality that one couldn't have imagined, no matter how much you'd read about war. I thought of a First World War poem that compared the sound of a shell to "a giant door slamming."

I hated the fear, but also found it interesting in a bizarre way. Controlling fear, real fear, is, if nothing else, a pretty fascinating challenge. I was always amazed that armies could successfully train people to endure combat for weeks on end — two hundred and fifty days is about the maximum that even the toughest units can stand — and actually train people to keep on working in states of near panic. It is like trying to function in a vice: the throat constricts, stomach rumbles, the skin goes clammy, the voice becomes a ridiculous squeak, the mouth becomes Sahara-dry in a flash, and seems to stay dry no matter how much water is guzzled.

In news, there are particular problems: you have to keep up a calm front before your own crew and other journalists, and, in television, you have to somehow will yourself to overcome your fear symptoms while on camera. But perhaps the worst part is that it's not a job where you have any particularly useful physical work to do while in danger. The military knows that physical tasks help ease a soldier's fear; television crews have more than enough to do when the going gets rough. But producers and reporters are often left standing around, uselessly clutching notebooks and pens, feeling both idiotic and terrified at the same time.

I've found that a lot of correspondents tend to glide gently over the subject of fear when they come to write their memoirs. But it's an inevitable ingredient of foreign correspondents' existence if they have to cover danger zones. All of us have seen colleagues who break or run under the strain, and normally they are not blamed. Some demand to be sent home. Some just quit. Others are rendered immobile and have to be removed for their own good. A few just get drunk and try to stay drunk. In a nuthouse like Beirut, a refusal to continue is often greeted with sympathetic nods by the journalistic community. It's a given there that the bizarre nature of the city will have different effects on everyone, and each person has to set his/her own limits.

There is often real anger, however, towards those who

volunteer for the glamour of working abroad but refuse to pay the price when things turn rough. One very famous American correspondent is reputed to have sniffed "I don't cover wars," when asked to do his news stint in Vietnam. His colleagues were neither amused nor forgiving — one is supposed to make such reservations clear before one takes on the job.

In news, you usually have to handle fear yourself. You don't have the camaraderie or cohesion of military units. I remember a quote from a British army psychiatrist, much experienced with combat, who was sent with Thatcher's expeditionary force to the Falklands. His job was to care for those who broke under the strain. Asked what types would give him the most problems, he replied: "That's easy. Reporters. They're always a problem. They're not working in tight-knit groups. They don't have buddies . . . in fact, they're competitors and don't even like each other that much. So, they have no support when the strain builds up."

True to his predictions, the media brigade that went with the troops became notorious for bitter infighting and intrigue. And very few distinguished themselves in the field.

NBC's **Henry Champ** *insists that bravery among journalists in the field is usually inspired by stupidity rather than nobility.*

I am often amazed at my own reaction to dangerous situations. Once, in Iran, a group of us were dropped on to an open road in the Fao Penisula by Iranian Air Force helicopters. As we hit ground, the Iraqi Air Force spotted us and sent over some jets. They didn't want any journalists around, so they began bombing. Shells exploded everywhere. A reporter from *Der Spiegel* was killed.

I ran to what was a kind of dugout and, as I ran, my passport fell. Although it is shocking to recall now, I actually stopped and ran back after it. I didn't know what I was doing. At the time it seemed an important thing to do. The guy I was with was shouting: "Henry! What the fuck are you doing? Come on! Come on! Come on!" But I went back to get the passport. Who knows why I did that.

But don't misunderstand — every time I've been shot at, it was a mistake. I've never gone looking for "bang-bang." I'm not a gunfire junkie. I'm terrified all the time. I am not a brave man. The only times I have encountered gunfire have been the times when I misdiagnosed the danger level and crossed the line. Nobody whom I respect seeks out gunfire. You only do that if you're sick.

In 1984, The Journal's **Linden MacIntyre** *was briefly, if reluctantly, conscripted into the Salvadorean civil war by an over-eager, adrenaline-charged producer. But while his producer may have been determined to capture scenes of brutal violence, known in the business as "bang-bang," MacIntyre was more circumspect.*

This is a story that illustrates a lot of what's wrong with what television journalists do for a living. We were down in El Salvador, covering the 1984 presidential election campaign. None of the crews at *The Journal* was particularly keen about going on this assignment because the producer was one of these guys who is addicted to spills-and-chills. No matter what story we went after, this man would figure out a way to go chasing guns. A lot of the crews wouldn't travel with him because they knew that, someday, somebody was going to get shot and the chances were it would be either the cameraman or the soundman. Producers never get shot.

Upon arrival, our producer revealed an immediate and total preoccupation with shooting the war in El Salvador, forgetting that we were there to cover the election. In no time, we found ourselves taking daily treks into treacherous hills, seeking out treacherous guerrillas, in the company of the most treacherous armed forces on the face of this planet.

On a typical day, we climbed into the back of a big truck, with a group of half-educated, psychopathic soldiers, drove along bumpy dirt roads until the roads ran out; then we hiked in a long column through woods, and across rivers, passing villages full of sullen and miserable people, waiting for the sound of the shot that was going to give us the tape that would make us famous.

Instead all we got was endless trudging, endless thirst, and, in my case, a stomach infection that required endless dashes into the brush. And we were getting nothing. Absolutely nothing. We searched the length and the breadth of the country, but people just refused to shoot at us.

In growing desperation, our producer went to an army base and had some consultations with the military brass. When he returned, he called a little meeting. "Okay, here's the drill," he said. "We're going to be helicoptered into a place that is effectively surrounded by guerrillas. About 150 army troops are trapped in the middle. They'll helicopter us in to join them, but they take no responsibility for what happens. Once we're in, we can't be airlifted out. We'll have to walk out. In all likelihood, it's going to be very dangerous. There's going to be shooting, and I feel obliged to offer you the opportunity not to go if you don't want to."

As the producer talked, the soundman's eyes just got wider and wider until he finally said: "I'm not going!" But Guy, the interpreter, and I, said, "Okay. We'll go."

So, we climbed onto an army helicopter at a time when Salvadorean helicopters were being shot out of the air with great regularity, arrived at the hilltop and were dumped out. We had no sleeping gear and no food, just recording equipment. So, we had a meeting with the commander on the hilltop — who reassured us we weren't going to be there long. Tomorrow morning before dawn, we will sneak down the hill. Great, I thought.

We curled up on the ground and tried to sleep on what was

possibly our last night on earth. At 3:30 a.m., a hand shook me awake. A soldier put his finger to his mouth saying only "Shhh." I noticed all these dark shapes as people began to assemble. We travelled down the hill in absolute silence. We crept along and eventually hit a dirt road. Occasionally we would hear the sound of a vehicle. Everyone would take off into the trees and wait until the vehicle went by. We snuck through the dark for miles. Slowly we saw the sun begin to come up, and I thought: Okay at least now we can see where we're walking. On the other hand, so can other people.

We were starting up a slope when we heard the first bang. We didn't know where the shot came from, but in a split second it was like World War Three. There was machine-gun fire, mortar fire, rifle fire, exploding grenades. I did a swan dive into the dirt, as did everybody except the people with the guns. I kept thinking that all this fire was going over the village we had just walked out of, full of nothing but women and children.

As soon as I got my senses back, I peeked out to see what Guy was doing. He was eating mud like I was. But he had the camera and was screaming at the translator, who, not being a trained soundman, had committed the supreme error of getting himself separted from us. After a lot of groping and straining, they finally got hooked up. The camera was turned on. But as soon as they stared rolling — whoosh — peace breaks out. You could hear nothing but the tweeting of birds. This, after days and days and days of struggle to get this sequence. The moment did happen, only not on camera. We spent the rest of the day walking to safety. The next day our producer suggested another safari. A vote ended that idea.

Whenever I asked a foreign correspondent to name the worst place on earth, the same spot kept being chosen: Beirut. It is the only assignment where journalists feel afraid all the time. Since the arrival of the PLO *in 1970, the Lebanese civil war, waged by various rival Christian and Moslem factions, has taken over 150,000 civilian lives and pounded a once beautiful, seaside semi-democracy into rubble. Western journalists have virtually ceased reporting from Beirut since the hijacking of* TWA *flight 847 in 1985. The threat of kidnapping and murder has become too great even for the most reckless of reporters and, as a result, the reports we receive now are filed — almost without exception — by local press. But, even from a distance, Lebanon remains the most grimly fascinating conflict in the contemporary world. It is in Lebanon that the terrors of the twentieth century have come to their culmination: total, unending, unresolvable, barbaric slaughter. During an early visit to Beirut,* CTV's **Jim Reed** *got a mercifully brief taste of what it is like to be held captive by young Lebanese fanatics.*

I spent two months in 1976, covering the civil war in Lebanon. The Christians and the Moslems, the left and the right, were all battling it out for control of Beirut. For a long time I believed a press card conferred some kind of immunity from violence. Two things happened that disabused me of this idea.

The first was seeing our Lebanese driver shot through the throat. Every day we would go out to the site of the fighting, get a feel for what was going on, do a stand-up, and send back a report. One time, I crossed the street with the cameraman, and asked the driver to stay with the car. I looked around and saw him running towards us. Suddenly, he fell down in the middle of the street. He had been hit by a stray bullet, which went straight through his neck.

We put him in the trunk of the car and, for the only time, I drove through the streets of Beirut. We took him to a hospital and miraculously he survived. He was not a lucky man, however. He died when his apartment building collapsed during the big bombardment of 1982.

The other experience happened on a visit to a Moslem community captured by the Christians. I was in a car with a photographer for the London *Times* and a stringer for NBC. We came to a checkpoint held by one of the Moslem factions. The boys at the checkpoint were maybe fourteen years old. They had bayonets stuck down in their boots, they were carrying machine guns, and had revolvers and ammunition strapped on.

I handed over my press letter. They looked at it and it was fine. The NBC stringer showed his letter and that was fine. Then the London *Times* fellow pulled out his letter, only he pulled out the wrong one. He mistakenly showed them his letter from the Kataeb, a Christian Falangist extremist group.

We were all dragged out of the car. They searched us and, of course, found all of our letters from all the different groups. We tried to explain that this is how journalists operate, that we had to get permission from everybody. They wanted to make it very clear to us that we shouldn't be dealing with Christian troops. Ten hours later they let us go.

This was just a foretaste of the kidnappings that started to occur a few years later. I just can't imagine what people who have been kidnapped have gone through. It was really the kidnappings that stopped me from ever going back to Lebanon. A news story just isn't worth it. The guy from the London *Times* came to the same conclusion. He left the country three days later.

NBC's **Henry Champ** *was in Beirut when word of the 1982 Israeli invasion began to surface. In tracking down the story in a small Lebanese border town, Champ made the nearly fatal mistake of standing a little too close to a suicidal young Lebanese warrior.*

I remember lying once up to my chin in slime and garbage in a sewer in Lebanon. Bullets were going off all around and I was sure I was going to die. Although I am an agnostic, I do remember promising someone, although I can't explain exactly who, that, if I got out of there, I'd never do anything bad again. I'd quit my job and become a priest. I did get out, but I didn't become a priest.

We were in the sewer because somebody had reported that the Israelis were beginning their incursions into Lebanon. From Beirut, we headed about forty kilometres to the Israeli border to see if the report was true. The Israelis were denying any activity. But we went to get some pictures that would prove that, at least on the day we were filming, they were there.

We came into the village and started asking around: "Have you seen anything? Or, to use their language: "Any Izzies around?" We met some armed Lebanese Amal people, none of whom was much older than twenty-two.

We went into a house to chat, and all of a sudden, we hear "rumble, rumble, rumble." A couple of Israeli tanks and an Armed Personnel Carrier were about five or six blocks away. They were in a valley and we were above them. Here was proof that the Israelis had been lying. I'm not making a moral judgement about what they were doing, but, from a reporter's point of view, it's a beautiful story.

We moved into the breezeway, and started filming. We were followed by about eight fifteen-year-olds. Suddenly, one of them took out an RPG [rocket-propelled grenade] and fired it through the trellises, hitting the Armed Personal Carrier. A shot like that is like throwing a spitball. It just bounced off the thing. Their guns turned around and, with more firepower than you can believe, they reduced the house to kindling.

It didn't take a genius to realize you had to get down somewhere or you were going to die. We all ran like hell and dove into the sewer, full of water, carrot roots, and garbage about a foot deep. We stretched out in this stuff. I stuck my face out just enough to breathe.

When the firing finally stopped — it seemed like three hours but was probably about three minutes — we climbed out of the sewer and skulked across the road. Once we were back to safety, I did something I have never done before or since. The fifteen-year-old who had shot the RPG had a big smile on his face. I hit him harder than I have ever hit anyone. I laid him out on the ground. I'm not a violent man but I was so hyped, so frightened, so terrified. The instant that thing went off, I thought: I'm about to die because of this kid's stupidity.

At the time, surprisingly enough, I was also thinking about the new jacket I had just bought. I know it sounds incredible but with all the fear that I felt and all the praying I was doing — God, please get me out of here, this is my last war zone, don't forget the wife and kids! — another part of me was thinking: Jesus, this new jacket cost seventy-five dollars!

Together with his colleague Ann Medina, former Journal *producer* **Gordon Henderson** *survived a Lebanese bombing attack, the target of which, terrifyingly enough, appeared to be the journalists themselves.*

Ann Medina, cameraman Jean-Guy Nault, soundman David Fox, and I had clearance to work in Israeli-occupied South Lebanon until three o'clock that afternoon. It was understood that everyone would turn a blind eye if we missed the curfew once, provided we were back at the border the next day at three o'clock.

We were dropped off along a deserted coast by the UNIFIL driver, and picked up by a man in a Mercedes.

We shot all day, interviewing people in Tyre, then rendezvoused with a Shiite leader who could best be described as a dispatcher for the suicide bombers.

That evening, we were the only guests in The Eliza Beach Hotel and the only people having dinner in a cavernous, main-floor restaurant. We went to bed early because we had a lot of work to do before the Israelis closed the border. I was fast asleep when the bombs went off. Assuming there was fighting going on nearby, I hurried out of bed to wake the others. That was pretty stupid. No one could have slept through the explosions.

The first person I saw was Ann, who said her windows had been blown out. The waiters from the dining room were now running along the corridor, saying everything was all right. We probably would have taken their reassurances more seriously if they hadn't been carrying machine guns.

We stopped the man who had checked us in, and Ann asked, "Where's the bombing?" His answer: "*Ici.*" We followed the hotel employees downstairs to the restaurant. It had been completely destroyed by bombs set in the garage under the restaurant.

Guy felt that, if those who set the bombs came back, it was likely that they'd throw grenades through the windows, so he slept on the floor. Ann stayed in my room. We passed the Scotch back and forth and flipped a coin for the bottle. I still have it.

CTV *news reporter* **Dennis MacIntosh** *describes the less-than-serene ambiance of lunchtime in Beirut.*

Everything you do in Lebanon is dangerous, even eating lunch. Tony Nayel, our driver, insisited we eat at his home at least once a week. He lived on the Green Line separating the warring factions, on a street with Christian barricades at one end, Moslem at the other. In between was a no-man's-land and that's where Tony, his wife, and three children lived. When we arrived for lunch, Tony parked across from his apartment building, warning us not to move until he gave the word. He explained we had to run quickly across the street, but not to worry because the snipers would not be able to aim that fast. He was right.

He lived on the second floor. The living room had bullet holes in the ceiling, and the glass in the windows had been replaced five times that year. You could walk out on half of the balcony, but the bullet holes beyond that suggested you not walk on the other half. As we settled down to chicken, salads, and pita bread, we talked to the sound of mortars, machine-gun fire, and sniper bullets finding other victims. We were never there when things were really bad.

The Journal's **Linden MacIntyre** *remembers Lebanon's suffering children.*

Journalists survive by carefully erecting shields of reserve around themselves. But, every once in a while, that last bit of reserve is attacked, especially in a place like Lebanon. For people who have grown up in societies where children are safe, you cannot help but be touched to see children who grow up in societies where they are in constant danger.

You try to reserve your sentiments and keep your emotions in check. And then you run into the children. One day we went into a hospital in Sidon. We were talking to and looking at victims of various kinds of violence — incendiary bombs, bullet wounds. I remember interviewing a little boy of about ten or eleven as he was lying on a bed, in a posture typical of little boys: his hands behind his head and his legs crossed at the ankle. Except, one leg had the foot missing. It just ended at his ankle. I asked him — what do you want to be when you grow up? He said: "I want to be a soccer player." He didn't even know his foot was gone.

We continued through the hospital. It was horrible. But we got our shots, and we got our interview clips. I was quite pleased with myself for getting through all of this. I didn't get sick. I didn't throw up. I went through it.

As we were leaving this awful place full of the stink of injury, I spotted a beautiful little girl by the nurses' station. She was just gorgeous. It looked as though she had become the pet of the world. She looked unscathed. She had big gold studs in her ears, and looked like a kid who had been very well cared for.

"Oh," I said, "who's she?"

The nurse said, "Oh, we think she's about four."

"Don't you know?"

"No," the nurse replied. "We can't find any of her relatives."

She had been discovered sitting on a heap of rubble that had been a home, just sitting there. Everyone else was gone. So, they had brought her in, and they kept her there. I squatted down in front of her, trying to communicate, and up close noticed big, bubbling beads of perspiration all over her face and a vacant look in her eyes. I couldn't get any registration there. And then I saw that she was all wrapped in a white blanket. Completely wrapped up, though it was very hot. So, I said to the nurse, "You've got her all bundled up. Look at her — she's perspiring. She's melting." And before the nurse answered, I opened the little girl's blanket. Her legs had been blown off right at her knees. In their place she had two little bandaged stumps. That's why they had her in the blanket. She was still in shock.

That was the end of me. I was finished. All the carefully preserved professionalism crashed. I got physically sick and just made it to the bathroom. Those are the moments that are hard to recover from. Every so often the touch is too heavy.

*If there ever was a reporter who was inexorably drawn
towards danger, it was* CTV*'s correspondent Clark Todd.
There was no place he wouldn't go, no question he wouldn't
ask, no closed door that he didn't want to open. In 1983,
when the brutal battles of the Lebanese civil war had
frightened off almost every other reporter, Clark Todd
insisted on wading deeper and deeper into this complicated,
calamitous story. Frantically pursuing the intimate details of
a war with which he was obsessed, he died during a shelling
of a small Lebanese village in the Shuf Mountains.
As* CTV*'s vice-president* **Tim Kotcheff** *explains, when he
and fellow vice-president Don Cameron first heard that
"something" had happened to Clark Todd, they immediately
hurled themselves into the task of saving him.*

It was a Sunday night when we learned that Clark had been
wounded. I was on a plane Monday. We thought he was still
alive, and we were in a hurry to get him out. But finding him
was not so easy. There were no flights into Lebanon. So, Don
Cameron and I split up. I went through Cyprus and he went
through Israel. In Cyprus, I caught a ferry to Beirut and I
arrived on Wednesday.

At this point, all anyone knew was that Clark was in the
Druze town of Kafer Matta, and he was wounded. There had
been a massacre of Falangists but continuing fighting between
Druze and Christians prevented anyone from going in.

The Christians held the neighbouring town, so I hung
around their headquarters in Beirut. I just sat in their office,
saying: "Look, I need to get up there." They were in the

middle of a war and the last thing they were worried about was accommodating me, although they didn't like it that a reporter had been hurt. What I didn't know, but they did, was that two hundred men, women, and children had been massacred and their bodies were lying around where Clark was. The Christians didn't want to let anyone into the area for fear of sparking an international incident.

They kept putting us off until they couldn't stand our pestering any longer. The PR guy for the outfit decided to be helpful.

After a two-hour, harrowing powerboat ride, we arrived at a power station on the coast, south of Damour. It was the safest place around because both the Druze and the Christians took their power from this plant.

I went in with Brian Kelly, Clark's cameraman, because he knew where Clark had been. I was expecting a military truck to pick us up, but our fixer pulled up in an old Opal and told us to slink down in our seats to avoid sniper-shooting. They always have the windows rolled down, so if the car gets hit, the glass doesn't fly all over the place. I don't know where the bullets are supposed to go.

We went for an incredible drive through Damour, where the PLO massacre of Christians that had started the wave of revenge killings took place. The whole town had been wiped out. We were taken up the mountain to the Falange headquarters located in an old school. On the second floor, they were interrogating people from Kafer Matta, asking them if they had seen Clark Todd. It looked like they were making a real concerted effort to find him.

The school was a target because the Druze knew it was the

Christian headquarters. When the first shell landed, I just about fainted. I'd never heard anything like that in my life. You felt a concussion.

Everybody was running — it wasn't just us. We huddled on the stairs. The shells would hit and the place would shake. Your skin would shake, the dust would fall. They rained on us. I was huddled with all the soldiers and, by chance, the guy next to me was from Montreal, a very devout Lebanese Christian. We talked about Canada because we didn't want to think too much about anything else.

One man slumped in the corner. I'll never forget his eyes — they were so piercing. He had lost half his family. I've never been that close to death. I was losing hope of ever seeing my own family again, when the shelling stopped around midnight.

The Christians had a truck at the headquarters, and I asked to use it to go get Clark. "Look, you don't understand this," they said. "If you think it's bad down here, there's much more shooting up there. There are snipers all over the place."

"But your people are going up," I replied, as I began to realize there was more to this than just our own safety.

Our fixer explained to us that, in any case, the only way to get a body out was in a Red Cross truck. "Go to the Red Cross," he told us, "and get a cease-fire."

"What do you mean 'get a cease-fire'? How the hell am I supposed to negotiate a cease-fire — these guys have been fighting for centuries."

But we did get a convoy organized from the Red Cross, which took us to a field hospital a few hundred yards from the fighting, about three-quarters of the way up the Shuf Mountains. A tank would roll in and throw some bodies out. It was a horrifying scene. The doctor would walk around, saying: "That's it. Wrap that one up. Throw him out. Dead. Next?"

The Druze would not agree to a cease-fire. They gave us twenty minutes to get out before they started firing. So, the Red Cross got us back down the hill at breakneck speed. New negotiations through the Red Cross would take days. We stayed in an Israeli camp in Sidon, sleeping in army barracks, trying not to give up hope.

In frustration, one night we did a foolish thing. We got a taxi driver in Sidon for a sum — a huge sum — to head up to this other strategic Christian stronghold.

The commander was very interested in our story, but the Christians were beginning to lose against the Druze counterattack and were facing extermination. We didn't know that, but they were clearly frightened for themselves and their families. When these guys clean out a place, they kill everybody, and the Druze had blood in their eyes.

So, back again to the Israeli barracks. We explored every lead, every rumour. We searched the main hospitals. We never stopped. We went day and night. We were working on adrenaline. I was never tired.

The next day, feeling utterly frustrated, we got another cab and said: "The hell with it! Let's just drive up there. This is bullshit. Let's just go." At Damour, a Lebanese Red Cross unit offered to take me up.

Don said, "Don't go with them! They are going to kidnap you. They're kidnappers."

I said to him, "You're crazy. I'm going. C'mon, let's go."

Don grabbed me by the arm and we started fighting. He

told me I was nuts. I replied, "Don, it's either this or we go home. We're accomplishing nothing. This is our last chance." Our fighting had frightened off the Red Cross, and our cab from Sidon. The poor old cabbie. Don ran and grabbed him and dragged along the road until he stopped his car and agreed to take us back to Sidon.

Eventually, the International Red Cross did send a convoy up, and our fixer said he would accompany them. In other words, they were now prepared to deliver the body. They said they were going to arrange a cease-fire and get Clark out.

I saw the Red Cross come down. The fixer came to us and said: "We've got the body, and he's dead. You have to make an identification." I went with them to a makeshift morgue. They laid out a bag and cut it open. I recognized his clothing. I had worked with him in Belfast, and it was the same outfit. We made the identification and I thanked them.

Later, we were able to piece together the story of what had happened to Clark. He was caught in the middle between retreating Druze and advancing Falangists. The Falange were shelling the town. He was hit and dragged into a cellar. He bled to death there.

Before he died, he drew a message in blood on a pillowcase saying that he loved his wife. She received it in the mail some time later, together with a letter from Druze leader Walid Jumblatt. In it, he said they'd found the pillowcase in the room with Clark and talked about Clark as a hero, saying he was shot by Christians for telling the truth. However, the autopsy report showed no bullet wound. And I didn't see a gun wound. His wound looked like shrapnel.

The Commodore Hotel, located in the Moslem section of West Beirut, off what was once the poshest shopping street in town, was headquarters to the busloads of foreign reporters who camped out in Lebanon during the early eighties. Its popularity was tied to its working telex machines, functioning telephones, proficient translators and fixers, late-night room service, and, perhaps most importantly, its well-stocked bar.
The Journal's **Linden MacIntyre** *describes the Commodore's charms and reveals how this alcohol-soaked institution survived as long as it did, unchallenged by its puritanical Moslem neighbours.*

I've always maintained that the most dangerous place in Lebanon was the bar of the Commodore Hotel. The bar was dangerous for two reasons. To relieve stress in Beirut, you couldn't exactly go jogging. So, you tended to congregate with your peers in the bar. The damaging and dangerous effects on the body, if not as dramatic as bullets and shrapnel, are almost as bad.

Moreover, the hotel was a liquor dispensary in the middle of an Islamic neighbourhood. At any given moment, Islamic fundamentalists might decide to erase this perfidy from their midst.

All that persuaded me, on one of my visits, to stay out of the bar. I went on the wagon. Yet, at the end of my stay, there was, to my astonishment, a charge of about $250 from the bar on my hotel bill.

When I complained to the front desk that I hadn't drunk

anything, they were a bit annoyed. "So what?" they said. "But, if you insist . . ." and the bill vanished. Shortly thereafter it came back cleaned up. No booze on it. I said, "Thank you very much," and paid it.

Only later did I come to understand the rather Byzantine accounting system of the Commodore Hotel. All was revealed when certain network officials, including the CBC, sent a delegation to meet with the management to find out what was costing so much.

The manager was straight out of a Graham Greene novel: sunglasses, slicked-back hair, mistresses, cigars — the whole package. He invited the executives on to the patio at the poolside and ordered up drinks and coffee.

"What's your problem?" he asked.

"Look," they said, "the price of staying here is extraordinarily high. It's higher than Paris. It's higher than the best hotels in London. And this is a very modest hotel."

The manager replied, "Well, it's understandable."

And they said, "Why is it understandable?"

He invited them to stop talking for a moment and listen to the "snap" and the "crack" and the "thud" of the guns and artillery you could always hear going off in Beirut.

"Don't you think it's unusual," the manager asked, "that in an environment like this we are able to sit here, under the open sky, by our swimming pool, drinking coffee and cocktails? You don't appear to be terribly worried. Do you feel safe?"

"Yes, we feel safe."

"Really? You feel safe?"

"Well, you invited us out here, so we assume it's safe."

"It is. But you should ask yourself why it's safe. Go out in front of this hotel and look across the street at the roof. You will see a couple of gentlemen with machine guns. They work for me. Survey the neighbourhood a little more closely and you'll find other people similarily outfitted who also work for me.

"I employ those people to assure myself, and to assure you, that nobody is going to drive a car loaded with explosives up this street and park it in front of this hotel. Or that gangs armed with .50-calibre machine guns are not going to take out half of the European and North American press corps.

"Sit in the lobby and keep your eyes open, and you will notice men coming through my office, with large canvas and leather bags. Examine those bags on their way out, and you'll discover that those bags contain money. I pay off an unusually large number of people not to come in here with their thugs, and their guns, and break up our bar and disturb the comfort and productivity of our guests, who work for you. So, the rooms and services in this hotel cost a little extra."

The network officials sat quietly, examining their drinks. Finally they stood up, shook the manager's hand, and went home, never to complain again.

As CBC *reporter* **Brian Stewart** *discovered during the Sudanese and Ethiopian famines of 1984, no reporter can behold such human misery and remain untouched by a desire to shake the rest of the world out of its complacency. He may arrive as a dispassionate journalist there to record a tragedy, but he can't help but turn into a sort of missionary whose goal is find aid for the suffering. Brian Stewart's reports on hunger in the Sudan and Ethiopia contributed greatly to the world's awareness. They roused such a wave of human emotion in the West that millions of dollars flooded into international relief agencies, and many lives were saved.*

A foreign correspondent is often torn by conflicting emotions. A part of one wants desperately to get to a crisis story, but another part dreads the experience. I spent weeks preparing for the Ethiopian trip: after weeks of war and famine there, we planned to move on to cover the escalating bloodbath in Mozambique.

I remember being preoccupied and tense. I felt at least mildly nervous every time the trip was mentioned. I was anxious to get going and cursed the long delays waiting for visas. Going into war zones — and Ethiopia has more than three of them — one is always vaguely aware that one could be killed, wounded, or captured. But there's also the certainty of sickness and, always, a merciless fatigue that would consume one's body and spirit for weeks on end.

I had never covered a famine, but had read a great deal about them and thought I knew what to expect. As a correspondent, I had always feared the development of what I called "psychic scar-tissue." In older colleagues, one detected a blunting of emotions, a deadness inside, that they'd developed after covering so much misery. Some were emotional skeletons, which always seemed to me an intolerable price to pay for one's career. Only later did I realize that experiences of horror can also alter a person for the better, and that sometimes it amputates spiritual gangrene.

My London news crew and I were pretty much burnt-out before Ethiopia. We were fatigued from long assignments in the Middle East. During the previous year, we'd had a dizzying ration of Lebanon — seeing the U.S. barracks in Beirut destroyed, covering whole city blocks shattered by car bombs, and witnessing too many mangled bodies in the streets. Our nerve endings were raw. We craved the excitement of new assignments, but the chaotic existence was taking its toll on our private lives. At home, in London, we were on constant alert, waiting for the phone call that would send us on the next dash to Heathrow and the beginning of the next challenge.

We all felt Ethiopia would tax us to our limits. A week before leaving, we vowed to keep in shape, watch our drinking, and generally "cover one another's back." I actually trained for Ethiopia . . . I knew it was going to be the gravest crisis of my career.

The Ethiopian famine from 1984 to 1985 was mixed up with war, so just getting to the worst-hit areas was a struggle. We had to fight our way through competing Ethiopian bureaucracies to get north to the famine areas, and then we only got there at all by hitch-hiking on relief flights.

The spectacle, as we flew towards the epicentre of famine

in Tigre and Wallo provinces, was of biblical proportions. Vast dust clouds drifted across a brown, sun-seared landscape. From ten thousand feet, we made out the long lines of famine refugees stumbling through mountain gorges towards the few food centres. Landing in the "High Roof of Africa," I thought of an astronaut's description of the moon — "magnificent desolation." All was ash dry and stark . . . the air, hot and windy all day, chilly at night. The cloudless skies swirled blazing stars overhead in the dark . . . one felt on a foreign planet, and as if one had passed out of time. I was mesmerized then, and am still, by northern Ethiopia, which resembles nowhere else on earth. Even the people wear the same peasant dress and till their poor lands with the ancient implements common in medieval Europe. I thought of Gibbon's description of the Ethiopians: "Cut off in their mountain fortresses, surrounded on all sides by enemies of their religion, so the Ethiopians lived for a thousand years, forgetful of an outside world that had forgotten them."

Reaching the famine, we overnighted in Korem, the small town dubbed by the BBC as "the worst hell on earth." We arrived at sundown and were promptly confined to a fleapit hotel, since rebels were marauding through the territory and Korem became a virtual no-man's-land after dark. We were forced to stay in hateful little rooms, which cost $1.25 a night, where we dined on tinned sardines from our food kits and huddled in filthy blankets as the hours crept by. But I could not sleep, knowing that people were dying by the dozens in the fields less than a mile away from us, and knowing, also, that I'd be visiting those fields when the sun rose.

Noises haunt me still. In the hours before dawn, I was

puzzled by what I thought were strange barnyard cries of animals that I couldn't identify. But, in the dawn, when finally released from the hotel, I saw that the noise came from small bundled bodies stretched along the road, begging for help or simply groaning in terminal starvation. For weeks afterwards, it seemed, wherever I went in the North, always on the ground before me were the small bundles, and the sound of life ebbing from them.

We entered the first famine camp at Korem at around 5:00 a.m., three hours before the medical staff were permitted to leave their guarded rooms. For that period we were the only outsiders in a camp of seventy-five thousand starving refugees. People brought their dying children to us, and we walked through stifling barracks as the gravediggers sorted out the dead from the living.

By 8:00 a.m. they'd piled up more than one hundred bodies — those who'd died during the night — in the small, green tent that served as a morgue. Other corpses lay scattered about the camp, which looked shockingly like a Nazi extermination centre without barbed wire or crematorium. Even the colours seemed monotone, as in a black-and-white newsreel. Ragged skeletons barely alive, huddled everywhere; women and children sheltered from the relentless wind beside the corrugated iron barracks in the famine huts where bodies lay three and four to a bed, the dead often intermingled with the living. Smoke from wood fires gave a hellish haze to the scene, and since there were no latrines for the seventy-five thousand people, one steppped through faeces and rubbish everywhere.

There were few sounds, only some moaning, and much

coughing from the crowds of refugees wracked by lung disease. Tens of thousands were to die of pneumonia inflamed by malnutrition. When bodies were collected, some relatives wailed, but even the voices of mourners were soon exhausted. The main sound was that terrible, dry wind that whistled through the camps and rattled the iron barracks that gave some pathetic shelter to the weakest in their dying hours.

We had imagined that famine would lead to food riots and violence. But famine has a terrifying calm face. Starvation, fatigue, and despair lead to a numbing of famine populations. The Ethiopians had a remarkable dignity — the strong did not shove aside the weak, rarely did anyone beg, theft was unheard of in the camp. But fatalism seemed to hang over the camp as thickly as the smoke haze. One wanted to scream out for those too tired to cry . . .

We were the only television crew in northern Ethiopia at the time. The BBC had come and gone a week earlier. Between October and February, ONE MILLION died in the famine. When we arrived, relief officials were warning that FIVE TO SEVEN MILLION lives hung in the balance. Massive aid had to begin pouring in within weeks. No one was optimistic. Aid volunteers were already in a state of collapse, even hysteria — One nun we worked closely with had a nervous breakdown and is still hospitalized in Britain. Everyone seemed braced for the worst disaster of modern times, and everything we saw seemed to promise still worse. The endless lines of refugees almost crawling in from the hills looked evermore famished; the death toll was growing at a stunning rate; the cattle were gone and many camps had no food. In Makelle, we arrived at one camp as the last ration was being distributed to thirty-five thousand people.

So, I felt I had a very clear objective: to help alert the outside world, and quickly. Our days seemed an impossible race against time. We were hurrying always to get our pictures, to write and do on-cameras, racing from one relief camp to another, from one rickety relief flight to the next. Ethiopia became a blur of food lines, refugee camps, funerals and more funerals, bodies stacked on bodies.

We were emotionally strung out, but also incredibly busy. And tired to the point our bones ached. In our first three nights in the famine zones, I had a total of two hours' sleep. For weeks I don't think I had more than four hours a night, and that was a very rare luxury. I lived on cigarettes, bottled water, and sardines.

While in the famine camps, we were so busy and so anxious to do the best work possible that the full emotional impact tended to be delayed. Like the aid workers, we were able to postpone the final reckoning until our work was done. But later it hit with the force of a tidal wave, stunning us as we sat in a luxury hotel in Addis Ababa, or dining out in London, or trying to sleep between clean sheets at home. For months afterwards, I had nightmares — images of starving children and corpses piled in the green tents. For a while, I slept with a light on to ease the shock when I awoke bathed in sweat.

Life became sadder and much more serious. One was nagged by guilt feelings when one's own life seemed so comfortable. Even the compliments that came to our Ethiopian coverage tended to backfire. One felt even worse.

I grew restless and increasingly dissatisfied with the reporter's role of "spectator." Since childhood, I'd devoured books about war and history, and later had viewed foreign reporting as a chance to take a ringside seat to history. But after five wars and four famines, after Ethiopia, everything else seemed a sideshow. I was rapidly consumed by the question: What the hell do I do about this myself? A long restless period led me to quit CBC and join NBC; I went vaguely looking for some new direction, but, of course, found none. Only after I returned to Canada was I able to start sorting it all out. There were documentaries, some private efforts to assist Ethiopians, and even the beginnings of some normalcy in life. But I still think of Ethiopia every day of my life and, if I have a second home, I now believe it's there.

Perhaps what oppressed me most was the sense of Life-as-Bully. I'd seen enormous suffering in many countries, but I'd never seen so much of it piled so mercilessly on so many innocent people. They faced every scourge imaginable — famine, war, economic collapse, plagues, tyranny, pillage, rape — pyramid upon pyramid of suffering. Beirut and El Salvador frustrated, frightened, and angered one. Ethiopia sickened one to the core, so unrelenting was the unfairness of it. But, at the same time, it drew one closer; its physical beauty and its people commanded involvement.

Another effect of Ethiopia, one rarely mentioned, was the extraordinary shock of seeing the world go environmentally amok. Television could portray the human suffering with some accuracy, but was unequal to the task of showing the collapse of the land. The drought area was a wasteland, similar, I suppose, to the dust bowl of the 1930s, a spectacle frightening enough to haunt forever all those who lived through it. I'll always see that massive sun hovering over northern Ethiopia, the land burned hard as concrete and swept night and day by the famine winds. This is what our world could look like if our environment fails. Sometimes, in Ethiopia in 1984, I had the eerie feeling I was peering into the future.

I expected our reports from the field would shock many people, but none of us anticipated the worldwide reaction. When it came, it overwhelmed us. I remember standing in that camp in Makelle that had run out of all food. Then, late one afternoon, I saw dust clouds erupting on the horizon, signalling the arrival of a long convoy of trucks, trucks carrying Canadian wheat. In the coming months we would see many such convoys, which estimates say saved around five million lives.

But all that said, it's worth noting the world reacted to the images of famine in Ethiopia, and not the fact of famine. The United Nations had warned of a great Ethiopia famine some months before it hit. Diplomats had been warned, governments alerted. But this early warning, along with a few press reports, went virtually unnoticed until the worst pictures came through on television. The hard fact is that the famine *simply didn't look bad enough prior to October 1984* to shake the world.

I used to be tormented by the fact that we couldn't get to Ethiopia sooner to help sound the alarm, but if we'd arrived two months earlier, our reports might have had little impact. The public needed to see famine before they believed it and reacted to it. By the time we see the images of a crisis, it is often too late. Famine is far too dangerous to be left to the emotional generosity of strangers. But, if anything good came out of Ethiopia from 1984 to 1985, it is that governments were burned enough by the scandal of Ethiopian famine to put new early-warning systems in place to guard against future famines. Barring an unprecedented environmental breakdown, I believe it is unlikely that we'll see another such famine for some time. Hopefully never again, for there's also increasing pressure on governments, including African ones, to tackle the worst food problems. Ethiopia scared the world into being more on its guard — because of it we may save countless millions in future.

Guilt, doubt, shame, and suspicion — The Journal's **Bill Cameron** *reviews the inner life of a foreign correspondent.*

Before the revolution in Mozambique, when the city of Maputo was called Laurenco Marques, the South Africans used to come to the Hotel Polana to play. Now the dining room is filled with reporters, diplomats, aid bureaucrats. The Polana is a little cusp of the First World in Mozambique: mahogany, brass, plush, marble, stiff white linen, ice cubes in crystal, cream soups, green watered grass — all in a country that does not seem to have struggled even into the Third. Mozambique is at the tag end of the Fourth World or the Fifth, whichever world is full of misery, cruelty, and starvation.

There are Polanas in every capital of every wretched, broken country in the world. The Camino Real in Managua is a Polana: a buffet with a band on Sunday afternoons beside the pool, a jogging path, and imported beer and satellite television in the lounge. The Sun in Gaborone, Botswana.

The diplomatic stores are even worse than the hotels. They're everywhere, the little caches of luxury that trade in hard cash, American dollars, British pounds, South African rands, travellers' cheques — no worthless cordobas or meticals, if you please.

In the centre of Maputo, the dollar store is a large building surrounded by armed guards and beggars. Inside, there is a treasure house of First World indulgences: Scotch, cocktail sausages, underwear, shaving cream, personal computers, butter, bathing suits, soap, Swiss army knives, Walkmans, videocassette recorders. When you walk through the door, you experience a kind of explosive compression. It's like being snapped around the world at the speed of light.

As I walked out the front door of the diplomatic store in Maputo with my soap and my salted peanuts, the beggars came towards me, and I waved them away. This was the professional thing to do. They seemed dismayed, angry, even more than disappointed beggars in other places; they were outraged, they roared at me. I walked through them and got into the car.

The interpreter explained that it was the custom on emerging from the diplomatic store in Maputo to give the beggars a box of crackers. It is their only food, their families' only food. For some reason, my little cruelty somehow seemed enormous. I felt a shame I have never felt before. The Fifth World had finally reached through and found me in the little mental Polana in which I travel.

That's the dreadful suspicion: that we dip into the surface of deep events, paddle with our feet, guard our comforts, patronize our contacts, exploit great tragedies for the good of our careers, and *get the story wrong.*

At three o'clock in the morning, in Room 1427 of the Polana Hotel, *that* often seems exactly what's going on. Maybe the real reporter is not necessarily the most talented, but the one who can survive all this guilt, doubt, shame, and suspicion, and get at least some part of the story home.

THE HOME FRONT

Though not as fatal as a blast from an M-16 or as terrifying as an unexpected midnight shelling, the poundings received by the men and women on Parliament Hill are severe, often bloody, and mesmerizing to watch.

Reporters who cover the "home wars" must produce combatants to tell us about their strategies and how the battle's going. Will the Liberals ever get their act together? Is the NDP finished? Who has Brian Mulroney's ear at the moment?

Not surprisingly, Canadians care far more about rancid tuna and Mulroney's shoe tally than the fate of the Burmese Revolutionary Guard. We follow the fortunes of our politicians as a form of public entertainment. Their drug habits, romances, and financial arrangements amuse us. We are titillated by stories that play to our over-riding cynicism about the process and the people who participate in it.

Politicians, no doubt, resent the invasion of television in their lives. But if nothing else, television forces politicians to abandon one of their more unattractive tendencies: inconsistency.

Before the days of a national electronic media, a federal politician might have campaigned in Quebec under a pro-Meech Lake banner, in Newfoundland under an anti-Meech Lake banner, and in Ontario under no Meech Lake banner at all — with no one the wiser. Today, such a tactic would be unthinkable. In the modern era, the unflinching eye of the camera ensures that when politicians lie, fudge, or contradict themselves the evidence will be there for all to see.

When CTV *correspondent* **Mike Duffy** *began working on the Hill for the* CBC *in the early seventies, he learned early from one of Parliament's great gentlemen that relations between the press and the Hill needn't always be nasty.*

People joke that in this town everything gets stamped "Top Secret," including — and I've seen it — newspaper clippings. It was Donald MacDonald who showed me my first top-secret government memorandum.

I was interviewing MacDonald in his office when a messenger knocked on the door and came in with a big, brown envelope marked "Secret." MacDonald excused himself, opened it up, and laughed. Then he handed the envelope to me. As a new boy on the Hill, I just about died! Here it is! My big moment — a top-secret memo placed right into my hands. It turned out to be a memo from the Clerk of the Privy Council saying that Louis St. Laurent had died (that was not secret) and they were canvassing for federal buildings or bridges — something in your department maybe — that they could rename after him.

I could have screwed him and reported: "Today Donald MacDonald opened a top-secret document for me . . ." But he wanted to help me understand the process. I was grateful to him for that insight. Politicians and journalists had a different relationship in those days.

When the Liberals abolished night-sittings of the House of Commons so that members could have a family life, they also abolished an important opportunity for casual social contact between journalists and politicians. During night-sittings, you used to be able to get ministers to come out to the lobby or press gallery, put their feet up, and explain why they were pursuing this and that policy. Now, relationships are much more intense, and much more adversarial.

It is during election campaigns that much of the bonding between politicians and reporters occurs. After six weeks of eating, drinking, and (metaphorically speaking) sleeping with each other, a reporter and his subject arrive at a new understanding. In the case of the CBC's **Wendy Mesley** *and Prime Minister Mulroney, Mesley learned just how quiet a man can be.*

In the election of 1988, I was on the prime minister's campaign plane. He sits up in the front, in the first-class section. In business class are his senior advisers. Then there's a curtain to keep out the rabble: his lowly advisers, the roadies in charge of the gear, and us — the reporters and technicians, who sit in the back and get rowdy. Mulroney came back to the rabble only twice; he didn't say anything either time.

The first time was the day we picked the name for the plane. A big war erupted on the two press buses between those who favoured "Pigs in Space" and those who preferred "Flyin' Brian." Finally we had to compromise and came up with "Non-commentaire."

Mulroney had heard us carrying out our unseemly competition on the intercom between the two buses. Shortly after boarding, he appeared holding up a sign that read: No comment. That was about as verbal as he got during the whole campaign.

Whenever it came time to get off the plane, Mulroney would wait until we were all outside, and then he would come out. The first week of the campaign they actually used white, plastic link chains to hold us back. Being herded like that made us breathe fire. We made appropriate mooing noises and sang "Working on the chain gang . . ." When we started writing the chains into our reports, the Tories caught on: this was not an effective technique. The white chains were quickly replaced with yellow cord, which somehow we found much less offensive.

On the campaign you work nineteen hours a day. Mulroney held up, but we reporters couldn't. He was always fresh, full of piss and vinegar. I think he's one of those people who can get by on four or five hours' sleep. There aren't too many reporters who can do that, even though we have all relinquished our terrible habits of the past — drinking, drugs, etc. You don't see much of that any more.

It's really quite a revolution. A boring one. We're all very serious now. We have so many more deadlines. You have to be on the ball all the time because, if something suddenly happens in the campaign, you *can* get it on the air immediately, or almost immediately. In the past, if it was eight o'clock at night, there was not much you could do. So, you would let go.

After weeks of hearing the same speech, something like Stockholm Syndrome sets in. You start thinking: Gee, isn't my guy amazing. He can perform so well, and people really do seem to like him. Or, you start to think: God! I can't stand this person! That's just as bad. You can't get too close, either in love or in hate. I must admit I was greatly relieved when my desk decided to have me follow Broadbent for a while.

CTV's **Pamela Wallin** (*who is married to CTV producer Malcolm Fox) on news, politics, and marriage:*

When you come off an election campaign, there are inevitably six marriages in Ottawa down the tubes. It's hard to know why, but it must be partly because, for seven weeks, you live on a high. You're on a plane every night. The hotel does your laundry. Everywhere, you walk with the leader, the crowds part like the Red Sea. You live on adrenaline.

The letdown when you come home is enormous. You go back to the same routine at work. Your wife or husband is talking about unimportant stuff. You're bored and want out. I attribute the success of my own marriage to the fact that we're both in the business and understand its demands. Malcolm put up with me through my years at Canada AM — our alarm clock would go off at 2:00 a.m. — and for that alone deserves sainthood.

CBC *radio and television reporter* **Jason Moscovitz** *resents that a reporter's dignity must often be shed to get his story.*

Brian Mulroney has changed a lot since he took office in 1984. He has become the master of the understatement. It started in the scrums six months before the 1988 election. He began whispering. If you weren't in the front row, you couldn't hear him. This guy, who used to be so full of bravado, who loved to argue, is all of a sudden almost inaudible. Scrumming him is now much more unpleasant and difficult.

For example, David Peterson comes to see Mulroney at 24 Sussex. I know, with Mulroney's new pitch, the only way I was sure to get the sound was to be at the front. So, there I am, with the prime minister of Canada, and the premier of Ontario. I am on my knees. I'm not alone on my knees. There's someone next to me on his knees and someone next to him — God forbid you stand in the way of a television camera. And I think as I hold up my microphone: This is not a great moment in my career. I took the sound, closed my eyes, and told myself: Not every day is a great day. And it will be over soon.

They had nothing to say and I knew they'd have nothing to say. My story sounded something like: "David Peterson came to see Brian Mulroney today. They said Meech Lake is very important. Peterson thought that it was very important Quebec be in it." Did I really need to be on my knees to understand that? Some believe it is really important to catch the spit out of politicians' mouths, like vacuum cleaners. I don't feel that way. On days when there is nothing happening in Ottawa — which happens a lot — you do get a little desperate. But, when you have to stoop so low to get so little, you feel you are only encouraging them.

While everyone would agree that indulging in excessive animosity towards a subject is improper, the journalistic code says sycophancy is worse. CBC cameraman **David Hall** *warns that overidentification with their subjects is a constant risk, especially for cameramen.*

I did the 1979 and 1980 campaigns with the Tories, and the 1984 campaign with the Liberals. I don't think I'll ever do another. You tend to drink a lot because the party is very good at making sure the plane is full of booze. And everywhere you land, there is beer: you tend to be half-buzzed most of the day. But the stuff you're shooting doesn't require any expertise — even though it looks like we were being pushed about, we always had guys from the party clearing the way for us.

The parties go out of their way to make you like their guy, to make you part of the team, especially when you're the cameraman. And, after a while, you start trying to make the guy look good. Joe was a nice guy but a nerd. He was not the easiest guy to make look good, but we tried really hard. He was someone I became very fond of.

Global TV's **Doug Small** *suggests that reporters usually cannot help liking the politicians they cover.*

I've been through a number of prime ministers, John Diefenbaker was still around when I started on the Hill. Mulroney is most like Diefenbaker. He loves to tell a good story and he loves to hear a good story, and, if anything, I think he's a bit frustrated by the constraints of being prime minister. His naturally gregarious tendencies have to be tempered from time to time.

One time, in the 1988 campaign, we were flying home from Saskatoon after two long, long days touring the Interior of B.C., Edmonton, Winnipeg, and all of Saskatchewan. We were coming back home to Ottawa and, needless to say, everyone on the plane was exhausted. But we were having fun and there was lots to drink.

One of the things I had in my little bag was a Mulroney mask. I put it on and was acting up in the back of the plane, when, who should appear at the front of the plane but Mulroney. As I was doing a Mulroney imitation at the back, he was doing a Doug Small imitation up front. So I said: "You're better at this," and I gave him the mask. It was the funniest thing I'd ever seen: Mulroney appearing from behind a curtain, doing an imitation of himself, leaning forward a bit and letting his hands dangle down in front of him — he has trouble with his balance — wearing a mask of his own face. He exaggerated all of his own characteristics. It was one of those moments that all reporters dream of — seeing the man behind the mask in the mask.

The CBC's **Don Newman** *on sources and anonymity:*

There are fashions in this business — right now it's that everything has to be in the open and on the record. The fact is, if you do that, you'll never learn anything. You'll just hear what they're prepared to say in the House of Commons. I don't mind taking information on a not-for-attribution basis. It's useful to know, for example, what a future budget is going to be like, even if I can't say who told me. It's good for me and its good for the public. This town is secretive, but people will tell you things if they know you're not going to use it right away.

The younger reporters who want everything on the record are kidding themselves. You don't get many scoops that way. The only danger is that if you take information off the record and it turns out to be wrong, you can't go back to the source and complain.

The media and politicians may see each other as natural adversaries, but as CBC's *Ottawa bureau chief* **Elly Alboim** *explains, a minister's real enemies are usually his colleagues.*

This whole town is a Turkish bazaar — everybody is trading bits and pieces of information. And when you start working the interdepartmental rivalries, you'd be surprised how easy it is to get information about department X from unrelated department Y.

Senior bureaucrats and politicans spend a good percentage of their time scouting out information that might impinge on them. The only place they can get that information is other bureaucrats or media people. They use us to find out as much about their neighbours as we use them.

The best source of information is very seldom the minister making an initiative. Primary sources are usually adversarial. You have to find somebody who is offside.

For example, during the process of constitutional repatriation, we found somebody who didn't like the way Trudeau was pulling ahead with unilateral patriation. He also didn't like the way he had been relegated to an inferior status in the process and was very happy to share with us. We got all the cable traffic between London and Ottawa and broke a large number of stories about it. It really freaked out the PMO.

Mulroney manages to keep more secrets than other prime ministers, but he cares more about keeping secrets. He regards it as a triumph if we don't know what the cabinet shuffle is the night before. If an appointee knows he'll lose the job if he goes public, chances are the information will remain secret. But the details of something like the MacDonald Commission on the Economy will always get broken the night before because so many people are involved and someone's bound to be offside.

For the guy who spills that story, it's a trading chip. He doesn't care about the Royal Commission on the Economy. He doesn't care if the prime minister gets his secret popped. What he does care about is his issue, and that the next time his issue comes up, that reporter will talk to him. It's a current-account deficit and surplus all over town. Individuals at the centre of things are bound by official secrets, oaths, witch-hunts, and all that. The trading goes on at the fringes.

During a time of excitement, when a source has to decide who to call back and who to talk to, he's going to choose the people he has an ongoing relationship with. If you don't maintain, at the very worst, monthly contact, but better yet, weekly or even daily contact with some people, you won't be able to do your job.

It becomes difficult to decide which story is worth rupturing a relationship. You always try to evaluate whether a story is of suffcient national importance or public interest to cause the sort of difficulties in communications that will jeopardize six or a dozen stories that are also in the national interest. We obviously reached that point with the story about John Turner's near leadership review in the middle of the 1988 election. It will take months if not years to re-establish relationships with a whole variety of people because of it.

In a federal election campaign, you don't need the same kinds of relationships. But you are playing a very long end-game in this business. If you violate confidences or understandings, even with the passing of the years, you are dead in the water.

The John Turner putsch story didn't violate the rules or burn sources. No single person had a sense of the whole. None of them understood they were doing anything particularly threatening or damaging because they didn't have the overall picture. When the overall story was done, a lot of people were taken aback and said, "I didn't really understand that I was participating in something that would ultimately damage the party. I didn't understand the implications."

Jason Moscovitz *explains that the reason he loves to cover politics is because it is "blood sport," in which the victors take all and the loser gets nothing. He recalls the day in 1976 when René Lévesque was sworn in as premier of Quebec, as Robert Bourassa was left to bleed alone.*

In 1976, when René Lévesque won the Quebec election, I learned a lesson about what power really means. I was in Quebec City, covering the transition period after the election. We were up in the press gallery when we heard the rumour that Bourassa had just resigned to the lieutenant-governor. We were told he was now in his private apartment in the Upper House — leave it to Bourassa to have his own apartment inside the Assembly!

We rushed from the fourth floor to the third, stood in front of the big padded door at the entrance of his apartment, and waited. Twenty minutes passed before the door opened. Bourassa looked shaken. He hadn't shaved in about three days. His collar was askew, his scarf crooked, his coat rumpled. He looked like a bum. He was stunned by the cameras.

On the landing, there was an elevator and a staircase. Bourassa looked at the elevator, realized he'd have to wait for it, and *ran* down the stairs. We ran after him. Outside, in the driveway, there was an old beat-up Pontiac with a driver. He got in and drove off.

We went back to our positions in front of the lieutenant-governor's office. Moments later, Lévesque strode down the hall to be sworn in. He had a big smile on his face and was surrounded by at least twelve people. Those five minutes, the person who was getting power and the person who just lost it, was the most powerful image I've ever experienced in covering politics. It's too easy to say that power is everything, but it is. That's all there is. The losers are always alone, although they always make a better story.

*There was a time once when nothing was funnier to
Canadians than a good Joe Clark joke.* **Pamela Wallin**
remembers that period with some distress.

In the 1979 to 1980 period, I really felt Joe Clark was being
maligned by the press. The criticism of his leadership was, by
and large, fair. But all that stuff about his lost luggage, which
we generated, bothered me. The guy was a decent person and,
God knows, that is rare enough in politics. You can't label a
guy a screw-up because he walks funny.

I found myself more sympathetic to Clark in the 1980
election than I otherwise would have been. After his defeat, I
followed him out on his first visit to High River. His press
secretary Jock Osler, his daughter Catherine, the pilot, and
myself were the only people on the plane. Nobody else
wanted to go on the trip.

It was Maureen and Joe's wedding anniversary that day and
she was flying in from Europe, where she had gone to heal the
wounds. Joe was standing in the backyard with some local
farmers, wearing his cardigan and looking awkward. When
Maureen arrived, there was this look of relief in Joe's face that
said: "Oh, my God, I really need a friend and an ally."
Everyone was being very nice to him, but he knew they were
thinking: How could you have blown this?

When you see that absolute vulnerability, you realize the
price they pay. It's easy for us to sit on this side of the fence,
criticizing. But they are just human beings and you realize
that's not what people want. People want to buy into the
myth that their leaders are special. Otherwise, why are they
leaders?

Pursuing stories of political corruption is an important but inelegant brand of journalism. CBC's **Jason Moscovitz** *had the job in the early years of the Mulroney administration. To his dismay and, no doubt, Mulroney's, he broke more stories than even the most partisan viewer could possibly enjoy.*
Moscovitz was one of the first to report on the Michel Gravel case, the Quebec MP *who was charged with fifty counts of influence peddling, bribery, and abuse of the public trust. He also followed the Oerlikon scandal, in which cabinet minister André Bissonnette was forced to resign. Bissonnette was charged with benefitting from the sale of land to a Swiss arms manufacturer that had recently been awarded a $600 million defence contract. The charges against the minister were later dismissed, but he did not seek re-election in 1988. After one year on the beat, Moscovitz called it quits to "avoid being labelled a little worm." A good journalist doesn't want to be immersed in slime for too long — chronic cynicism is a condition that must be watched.*

I did the dirt-beat for *The National* in 1986, a good year for dirt. With dirt stories, one thing leads to another. I stumbled on to the Roch LaSalle scandal while working on the Michel Gravel case. A lot of business people who paid Gravel but never got anything out of him wanted revenge, and they took it out on LaSalle. LaSalle had already fired one of his political aides after reports of his criminal record and links to the Montreal underworld. But the most damaging element of the story came when I discovered that some people had paid five thousand dollars to go to a party to discuss with LaSalle how to get government contracts. As well, his friends were taking five per cent commissions on contracts.

The story broke a month after Oerlikon and not long after the resignations of Robert Coates, Sinclair Stevens, Suzanne Blais-Grenier, and John Fraser. There's no question that Roch LaSalle lost his cabinet job because of my story. So, I can say, "Yeah I was responsible for a cabinet minister losing his job." But, given his record, it was rather easy picking.

I used to think that doing these stories were fine, and even some fun, but they are also a form of Russian roulette. You can be right twenty times, but be wrong once, and your career is over. We were very careful not to make any mistakes. Everything was checked twenty-five times. The final product was invariably only ten or twenty per cent of what we knew. We were overcautious and I didn't like that, but I always kept in mind the danger of going over the line and of being set up.

But one story that was absolutely clear-cut was the Brewery Mission story about the drunks who voted for Mulroney during the 1983 leadership.

It was late March 1983, and we went to Montreal for a series of delegate-selection meetings being held that weekend. The first was on a Friday night, in the Greek section of town. It was absolutely insane: people were locked out, people were screaming, people who didn't speak English or French and couldn't have understood a word of the proceedings. They were obviously there because they had been paid. It was the craziest meeting I've ever attended.

When it was all over, somebody from the Mulroney campaign came up to me and said: "Tonight was our Greeks against their Greeks. On Sunday it's our drunks against their drunks." I wouldn't have thought anything of it except five minutes later, someone else came said, "If you're staying for the weekend you should really go to the meeting in St. Jacques. It's going to be much more wild than this."

Two people in five minutes were telling me something. What was the message? Drunks? St. Jacques? The Brewery Mission was in St. Jacques. And if you're really going to play dirty, well . . . It was a long shot, but why not?

On Sunday, as we arrived at the mission, people were beginning to get on a school bus. I introduced myself to the guy who seemed to be in charge. I told him I didn't know where the meeting was — didn't — and asked if he would give us a lift. He said, "Sure." I got on the bus and asked, "Excuse me, are these Clark supporters or Mulroney supporters?"

He said, "We only have Mulroney supporters here." I loaded on the tripod, lights, and camera, and we started taking pictures. We knew right away what we had here, unbelievable as it was.

When the bus stopped, we got off first and shot everybody as they got off. I didn't interview anybody until the last guy got off, so as not to ruin the shot. The last guy was off in outer space. He didn't know where he was or what he was doing. He told us that somebody had given him this card, but he had no idea what the meeting was about. That clip was used over and over again because it was just so funny.

After the meeting, I was approached and told about a news conference at Mulroney headquarters. It was the first I'd heard of it, but I went. When I got there, there was no conference. I was taken into an office and handed a phone. Mulroney was on the line. We didn't talk about what I had.

He just talked about how everybody was missing the story of Clark's people beating people up with baseball bats on the South Shore. It was a very strange conversation.

Global TV's **Doug Small** *did not have to chase down the scoop of the decade. It came to him. All he had to do was open the door and say, "How do you do?" When Small announced the details of the Conservative government's 1989 Federal Budget one day before its scheduled release, he sparked a constitutional crisis that left many wondering whether Finance Minister Michael Wilson was obliged to resign. And, while he admits that he enjoyed the fracas that erupted as a result of the leak, he insists he feels little journalistic pride . . . it was all just too easy.*

I don't know what the legal constraints about talking about the budget are, I tend to just blather about everything. That was the easiest story I have ever done in my life. It just dropped into my lap. I can't go around making the case that this was the culmination of an illustrious career. It was a phone call. If I am to be praised for anything, it was that I got it and knew what to do with it quickly. And I suppose experience helps there. But, in terms of the story, good heavens, it was a summary of the budget. If I had received the whole thing, I probably would never have got it on the air because it would have just confused me. But, because it was nice and short and succinct, all I had to do was paraphrase it and there it was.

The Mounties claim I knew that I was commiting an illegal act, but it never occurred to me. If you can get information about a budget in advance, obviously it's circulating publicly. And that means that, if it falls into the hands of anybody who knows anything about money markets, they can make enormous amounts of money on the advance information about changes in public monetary and fiscal policy. In that situation, there's only one thing a reporter can do — get it on the air as fast as possible. Because as soon as it's out, everybody's on the same playing field again. So, it never even occurred to me to question whether or not I should do it.

My source called local television station CJOH first and asked for money; they said no, they didn't pay for stories. When he first phoned Global, we said the same thing. But the guy he was talking to at Global, Paul French, kept him on the phone and kept getting information from him. I gather because it was getting late — we're talking about five o'clock at night and the budget was going to come out the next day — the guy realized that it was about to be a dead issue, and so the question of money didn't come up again. When he talked to me, it was just a simple matter of arranging to pick up the information.

When I got the thing, I riffled through it and realized the submarine program had been sunk, taxes were going up, and the million and one things in the budget that were all news. How the guy got it was not, to my mind, the story. The story was the information. That was what I was interested in reporting.

I really wish I hadn't been charged with a criminal offence. It's a real pain to be dragged through the criminal courts system and its costing my company money and it's taking a lot of time — all, I think, for nothing. But I do not regret what I did.

The only complaint Global had was that I looked too smart-alecky when people would interview me. I had this great story and I was as happy as a clam that I had it, and so I gave this impression that I was a smart-ass. They would have been happier if I had been a little more restrained, but, Christ, I was happy. I felt lucky.

In the newspapers, people compared me to Second World War spies, a person who would sell out his country for glory. Generally speaking, these people felt I had embarrassed the government. They were annoyed by my demeanour as much as by the act. I felt I had all the scruples in the world, of course, but they were saying the opposite. But it didn't get me down because I realize it's part of the job. You can't be in the business and not be attacked periodically.

CTV's *chief Ottawa correspondent* **Craig Oliver** *has worked on both sides of the American-Canadian border and believes that, when it comes to spilling beans, Yankees do it better.*

The Americans make themselves so much more available than Canadians. A lot more. And the Canadians get burned that way. They always do. Because the Americans know how to get out their side of the story. The Canadians will say: "Well, we don't want to discuss this, and no, we don't want to discuss that." While the Americans say: "Oh, sure, here's what's going on." And when they're telling you what's going on, they're giving you their own spin. Canada always gets hurt in these sort of things.

Still, there is dramatically more access here than when I left Ottawa in 1980 for Washington. Reporters being able to go up to the lobby of the House of Commons and interview any member of the Cabinet walking through is unprecedented in my experience on the Hill. In the Trudeau era, they'd throw you out so fast, if you even thought about it.

Throwing questions to the prime minister was impossible. Not allowed. You would say to him: "With grace and favour, would you mind coming downstairs to the basement [studio] and talk to us?" The guy could say yes or no, and that was it. He would do it occasionally. Of course, the opposition did it all the time. Now if the prime minister says no to us, we put that on camera.

*James Keegstra, ex-mayor of Eckville, Alberta, will be
remembered as one of our nation's more notorious politicians.
His virulent anti-Semitism shocked and dismayed the nation.
Once exposed, he lost his job, both as a high school teacher
and as mayor. The Journal's* **Linden MacIntyre** *was one of
the first to interview him.*

My interview with James Keegstra did two things. First he
offended me with his message. And I was appalled, as I
became aware halfway through that shoot, of the impotence
of the media. He was using us as a platform. He didn't care
what we thought of him.

Bring in your cameras, sit down, ask him questions. He
answers them, then you go out, you broadcast them, and
people hear his answers. And some people say: "Gee, that's
terrible!" But a lot of people say: "Hey, that sounds logical to
me."

The first thing that surprised me was his willingness to be
interviewed. I hadn't thought this assignment would ever get
off the ground because he couldn't be crazy enough to do an
interview with us on this subject. But the guy said, sure.

He was the mayor of Eckville at the time. He said, "Let's do
it in the town hall." We did. I asked him questions and, to my
astonishment, he answered, elaborating on his nutty philosophy. When we completed the interview, I thanked him and
said, "We'll want more time with you." He was so full of
himself, he said, "Sure. I'm at your disposal."

So, we went out for a coffee — the producer, the crew, and
I. And I said, "I don't want to put that on television." I had

gone out there assuming that he would be a little bit embarrassed about what he was saying. But then I realized, of
course, he's proud of what he is saying and of his own
eloquence. He's delighted at having this attention and this
platform.

Finally I said to the producer, "We've got to do this again.
That interview didn't work. I was too polite. I want to do the
interview in his own living room, because what I want to do to
him should be done on his turf."

The danger in this business is the tendency in the audience
to identify with the guest. They see the guest as a person in a
strange milieu. And when the television person becomes
aggressive or rude, the audience member thinks: Gee, that's
not nice. They bring this person into their place and now
they're being rude to them! What rotten hosts! But if I am
rude to him on his turf, they know he has the privilege of
throwing me out.

I spent a couple of days worrying about my second interview, interviewing kids, parents, and the school principal.
The principal was probably the most chilling person I met
because he represented the kind of indifference and stupidity
that had permitted Keegstra to thrive in this system for all
those years. "My daughters went to his class," he said, "and I
helped them with their homework and I didn't see anything
wrong with it!"

By the time I got back to Keegstra, I was horrified. My first
reaction had been that this guy is so far out to lunch, it must
be obvious to everybody. But it turns out that people see him
and think: Well, if he says all that on television and he's so
comfortable with his beliefs, there must be some truth to

them. So, I said to myself: This can't be an interview, it has to be a mugging. This guy deserves to be beaten up.

I didn't realize how easy he was going to make it for me. I went to his mobile home. It quite nicely set up and there were two comfortable rocking chairs. He was dressed comfortably in a plaid shirt. He was just so much at home.

He had gone through his library and pulled out all his favourite books and stacked them on his coffee table. He had a huge collection, just the worst trash you could imagine. He had obviously been on the mailing list of every crackpot group in the world. I went through it all and thought, boy, this man is not an isolated phenomenon. This guy is part of a system.

By the time the camera went on, there was no more politeness. My questions were more like statements. "You have taught this . . . Who told you that?" And he'd start to answer and I'd interrupt and say, "But that's a lie. That's hate-literature." "No!" he'd say. "It's not hate-literature." But I'd never let him complete anything. He'd just get wound up and I'd interrupt him and tell him he was lying. I asked him: "How can you teach kids that the Jews killed Abraham Lincoln?" "Well it's true!!" he said.

My interview was a prosecution. But he thought this was a good, friendly debate between himself and this inferior reporter. The guy was totally formed by what he had read. That he had absolute self-knowledge made it all the easier to beat him up. I just went at him and at him and at him.

When we returned to Toronto, we made a devastating error in our editing. We used too much of Keegstra speaking and not enough of my prosecution because we were uneasy with my aggressiveness. When we screened the piece for the folks here at *The Journal*, there was a ripple of dismay. They felt that we had given this guy yet another platform. It's never happened to me before or since, but the documentary supervisor asked to see the field tapes of our interview with Keegstra.

We watched the whole forty or fifty minutes. They said, "That interview is the story. *That's* what we want on television." We re-cut the piece and put in chunks of the interview because what had happened in his living room was an event. It was a confrontation between his view and the indignation of the normal world.

I didn't represent the indignation of the Jewish people or of a persecuted minority that would be particularly offended by him. I had come to represent the collective indignation of normal people talking to a screwball.

Once we put it together again, everyone thought it was fabulous but would have to be "lawyered." I was against having it lawyered. It didn't matter if it was libellous or slanderous — it was *supposed to be* libellous and slanderous. Every now and then you deal with someone for whom the rules do not apply. With Keegstra, you play according to his inverted system and you whip him at it.

But it had to be done. I went in with trepidation, sat down with the documentary supervisor and the lawyer, and we played the film. At the beginning, the lawyer was scribbling furiously. Then she scribbled less furiously, and finally she put her notebook down and just watched it. At the end of it she was weeping. She said, "We shouldn't broadcast this. But we must." And the piece played untouched.

JEAN-GUY NAULT: A TRIBUTE

In October 1985, I flew to New Brunswick to be with Guy. His wife, Jill, led me into the intensive-care room. He lay there in traction, stiff, unmoving, staring up towards the ceiling. I leaned into his line of vision, but the eyes I saw weren't Guy's. They were distant, glassy, and heavy from drugs, pain, and worry.

The voice was all Guy. He mumbled — he always mumbles — "How's Pam?" My wife was due to deliver our third child any day. We talked about that for a while. Then he wanted to know how things were at the office. He was particularly worried about a friend who was having problems. He didn't want to talk about himself. Even as he lay in intensive care with his neck broken and his future uncertain, he was concerned about other people.

That's Guy Nault. Friends like Guy are hard to find. And this book attests to the many friends Guy has made across the country during his distinguished career as a news editor, news cameraman, and documentary cameraman.

Good cameramen are a rare breed. They blend technical skills and the visual arts, a journalist's knack for storytelling and a sniper's eye. They must be able to react in split seconds to changing, unpredictable events, and make it look as if they'd had the luxury of spending hours lighting and blocking the scenes. Directors and field producers make improbable demands, expect the impossible, and cameramen deliver. It never ceases to amaze me.

Guy Nault added his own special touch to every story he worked on. Because he's such an avid reader of newspapers and magazines, his editorial suggestions and advice are always valuable. His deep involvement in the stories gave him a great advantage behind the camera. He knows what shots to go after and how to compose a picture in a way that will guide the script along. You see, Guy wasn't just shooting images, he was recording life experiences.

Take his camera work on a *Journal* documentary called "Anna's Place," about a woman who cared for street people. Guy recorded more than pictures — we felt the mood of the place. He was terribly depressed after we covered the drowning of schoolboys in Lake Temiskaming in the late 1970s. He questioned the intrusion of the cameras into people's private grief. I think his camera work always expressed that kindness and thoughtfulness.

But he could be dogged when chasing a story. I think back to scrums on Parliament Hill when Guy bashed elbows with the best of them, or ran down the street to get the extra interview "clip." It's a competitive business and Guy is a fierce competitor.

These days, Guy is preparing for a new career and looking ahead. The watchful cameraman's eye will make him a great director or field producer. Sure, he'd rather be on location with his camera. Of course, he yearns to walk again.

Someone in a wheelchair once told those of us who are "able-bodied": "You sit on a chair in one room, then get up and walk into another room, where you sit down again. I do the same thing. I just stay sitting down." Guy hasn't changed; he's just sitting down.

Not long ago Guy said, "I don't like it, but I'm not going to let it get me down." And he hasn't. Why not? Because of something deep within him and some extraordinary people around him.

Jill Nault's strength of character, her courage and, most of all, her love have made Guy one of the luckiest people I know. Since his accident, Guy, Jill, and their children, Richard and Lisa, have pulled together and risen above difficulties that would have overwhelmed so many of us.

Guy, Jill, Richard, and Lisa — you've taught all of us about the great strength of the human spirit. Thanks.

Gordon Henderson

THE CONTRIBUTORS

CLAUDE ADAMS started his career in journalism with the Sherbrooke *Record*. As a reporter for Canadian Press, he was the first reporter to bulletin the imposition of the War Measures Act. In 1980, Adams moved to television, joining *Global News* in Toronto and, two years later, CBLT, CBC's Toronto station. He has been on staff with *The National* since 1984.

ELLY ALBOIM began his fascination with the news as an undergraduate reporter for the *McGill Daily*. He was hired by CBC-Montreal in September 1970, one week before the FLQ crisis. He moved to Toronto and *The National* in 1976. In 1977, at the age of thirty, he became *The National*'s Ottawa bureau chief. He has covered over two dozen Canadian elections and countless First Ministers' meetings. He is also an associate professor at Carleton's School of Journalism.

TOM ALDERMAN was born in Toronto and, during a long and distinguished career as a magazine writer, has written for almost every major Canadian publication. He joined *The Journal* in 1981 as a documentary producer/journalist specializing in sports.

MARC ALLARD was a soundman in the Ottawa bureau for CBC's *The National* from 1977 to 1985. He is now an editor at the CBC's Washington bureau.

ALISTER BELL has worked as a sound-recordist for the New Zealand Broadcasting Corporation, the Australian Broadcasting Corporation, and the BBC. He moved to Canada in 1970, and is currently on staff at *The Journal*.

JOHN BIERMAN was born in London, England. He spent fifteen years as a correspondent for the BBC from 1966 to 1980, covering Teheran, Jerusalem, Cyprus, and Northern Ireland. He is currently senior foreign-affairs writer with *Maclean's* and the author of a biography of Napoleon the Third.

DAN BJARNASON began his career as a reporter for the Toronto *Telegram* and later worked for the Regina *Leader-Post* and Canadian Press. From 1978 to 1981, Bjarnason was the foreign correspondent at CBC's London bureau. He has been based in Toronto since 1983.

HILARY BROWN grew up in Ottawa. When she was hired by ABC in 1973, she became the first female foreign correspondent in America. She was initially based in London, and later reported from Paris, Tel Aviv, and New York. In 1984, she returned to Canada to become anchor of Toronto's supper-show CBC *at Six*.

PATRICK BROWN moved to Canada from his native England in 1970. He worked as a reporter for CBC-Montreal during the pivotal year of 1976, and became *The National*'s Montreal correspondent from 1978 to 1980. Since 1980, he has been *The National*'s and CBC-Radio's London correspondent.

BILL CAMERON was born in Vancouver, British Columbia. He began his broadcast career as a free-lance for CBC-Radio. During the next several years, he also worked in print, as an entertainment columnist and editorial writer for *The Toronto Star*, and as associate editor of *Maclean's*. He became the chief news writer for *Global News* in 1973, and later became the anchor/commentator for *Global Newsweek*. In 1978, he became the anchor for CITY-TV *Ten O'Clock City-Pulse News*. He joined *The Journal* in 1983.

HENRY CHAMP joined the Brandon *Daily Sun*, his hometown paper, as a twenty-two-year-old sports reporter in 1960. In 1967, he joined the CTV *National News* in Montreal. Later, he became bureau chief for CTV in London and then Washington. He became a host of CTV's weekly current-affairs show, *W5*, in 1980. In 1982, Champ moved to the American network NBC to report from Frankfurt and London. He is currently NBC's congressional correspondent in Washington, D.C.

MIKE DUFFY was born in Charlottetown, P.E.I. He was an Ottawa parliamentary correspondent for CHUM-Radio, and later, CBC-Radio, before joining *The National* in 1977. He became host of CTV's *Sunday Edition* in 1988.

ALAN EDMONDS was born in London, England. He spent twenty-five years as a foreign correspondent for the London *Daily Express*, the New York *Tribune*, and *The Toronto Star*. He was host of CTV's *Live It Up* from 1977 to 1989.

MALCOLM FOX moved to Canada in 1966 to work as a film editor for the CBC. He was a news editor with CFTO for three years before becoming CTV's London bureau soundman in 1974. He served as a cameraman at CTV's Washington and Halifax bureaus. Since 1983, he has been a field producer with CTV's news program *W5*.

WHIT FRASER's birthplace — Merigomish, Nova Scotia — "is not even on the map." Fraser joined the CBC's *National Radio News* in 1978, reporting from St. John's, Newfoundland. In 1981, he moved to Ottawa to join CBC-TV's *The National*. His enchantment with the Canadian North began during his years in Ottawa and continued during his years as Edmonton correspondent from 1986 to 1989. Currently, he is the host of *Newsworld*'s "This Country."

BARBARA FRUM grew up in Niagara Falls, Ontario. In the early sixties, she started her career as a free-lance writer and commentator for CBC-Radio. She moved into print as a television columnist for *Saturday Night* magazine and a radio columnist for *The Toronto Star*. She became host of *As It Happens* in 1971, where she stayed for ten years. In the spring of 1981, she became the host and interviewer for CBC's *The Journal*.

ALAN FRYER was born in Cairo, the son of a British officer, and lived there until the age of ten. He joined the CBC in Montreal in 1977, reporting both local and national news. He moved to CTV in 1983 as an Ottawa political correspondent and covered two federal elections. He became CTV's Moscow correspondent in 1989.

HANA GARTNER was born in Prague. Her career as an interviewer began with CJAD-Radio in Montreal in 1970. She spent one year in Ottawa as a parliamentary correspondent for Standard Broadcasting before going on to host a variety of publics affairs and supper-hour shows in both Montreal and Toronto. In 1977 she became host of *Take 30*. In 1982, she began her eight-year run as a host of the *Fifth Estate*.

BRUCE GARVEY moved to Canada from London, England, in 1960 to report for the Pembroke *Observer*. He later worked for UPI and *The Gazette* in Montreal before landing at *The Toronto Star* in 1967. At the *Star* he served as city editor, national editor, and Ottawa and Washington bureau chief. He became the executive editor of *Global News* in 1978. In 1981, he joined *The Journal* as a producer/journalist.

DAVID HALL joined the CBC in 1960 as a cameraman for CBOT (CBC) in his native Ottawa. He moved to *The National* in 1976 as an Ottawa bureau cameraman and has been with the Washington bureau since 1985.

GORDON HENDERSON joined *Global News* in 1974 as a parliamentary correspondent in his native Ottawa. Four years later he moved to CTV's *W5* as a field producer. In 1983, he moved to *The Journal* to produce some of that show's most remembered reports from Lebanon. He returned to *W5* briefly to serve as senior field producer before becoming a founding partner of 90th Parallel Productions in Toronto, an independent TV and video production house.

ROBERT HURST was born in Toronto. His career in television began with a job as an overnight news writer for *Canada* AM — "The lowest paying job in the industry." Later he moved to Toronto's CFTO, CTV's local affiliate, as a city hall reporter. In 1976, he was promoted to the position of news director. He moved to CTV's *National News* in 1979, first, as producer and line-up editor, and later, as bureau chief in Edmonton, Halifax, and China. He served as a parliamentary correspondent in Ottawa before he became CTV's Washington bureau chief.

TIM KOTCHEFF has spent twenty-three years in television as a news and public-affairs programmer. He joined CTV in 1976 and is currently vice-president of CTV news, features, and information programming.

LINDEN MACINTYRE was born in St. Lawrence, Newfoundland, and raised in Port Hastings, Cape Breton. A native Gaelic speaker, his accent is probably the most distinctive on the CBC. His reporting career began with the Halifax *Herald*, where he served as the Ottawa correspondent from 1964 to 1966. His first work for television was as a story producer/ journalist for a CBC Halifax public-affairs program. Shortly after, he became host of *The MacIntyre File*. Since joining *The Journal* in 1981, he has reported from Central America, Europe, and the Middle East.

SHEILA MACVICAR began her CBC career as a reporter with the local newsrooms in Montreal and Calgary and frequently contributed to *The National*. In 1982, she moved to Toronto as a writer/reporter for *The National*. In 1983, she became a Toronto-based reporter for *The National*. She moved to *The Journal* in 1985, as a field journalist. She became a host of the *Fifth Estate* in 1989.

PETER MANSBRIDGE was born in London, England. He began his CBC career in 1968 in Churchill, Manitoba, where he helped develop the CBC service to the North. In 1971, he moved to Winnipeg as a reporter for CBC-Radio and, the following year, joined the local CBC television affiliate as a reporter. He became *The National*'s Saskatchewan reporter in 1975 and was assigned to the parliamentary bureau in Ottawa in 1976, where he remained for four years. He became chief correspondent for CBC-TV and anchor in May 1988. He is also anchor of *Sunday Report* and CBC Television News Specials.

DENNIS MCINTOSH was born in Winnipeg. He joined CTV in 1969 as a reporter first in Toronto, then Montreal. Between 1982 and 1986, he was news reader and an interviewer for *Canada AM*. He hosted CTV's *W5* for five years. He served as the CTV national news bureau chief in Washington and Peking, and is currently the associate producer of the CTV *National News*.

TERRENCE MCKENNA was born and raised in Montreal. He joined CBC-Radio in Montreal in 1976 as a researcher for the current-affairs program *Midday* and later moved to CBC's *Sunday Morning* as a field producer, focusing on Quebec politics. He joined *The Journal* in 1981.

ANN MEDINA began her journalism career as founder of her high school newspaper in Chicago, Illinois. She was a reporter for NBC-Cleveland during the early seventies, and moved to ABC–New York as a correspondent for *The Evening News* in 1973. In 1974, she was sent by ABC *News* to cover several Canadian stories, and it was on this trip that she decided to stay in Canada. She joined *The Journal* in 1981. She left journalism in 1987 and is currently an independent film producer, living in Toronto.

JIM MERCER was born in St. John's, Newfoundland. He started at CBC in 1967 as the first cameraman for *This Hour Has Seven Days*. In 1970, he moved to CTV to become a field cameraman for *W5* and has remained with the network ever since.

WENDY MESLEY's first experiences with professional journalism were with CKFM, CFRB, CHIN, and CHUM-Radio stations in Toronto, where she worked as a newscaster and reporter. She moved to television to become Montreal bureau chief for CFTO, the Toronto CTV affiliate. During 1979 and 1980, she worked for CFCF television in Montreal as a reporter and a co-host of their local current-affairs program. Before joining *The National*'s Ottawa bureau in 1986, Mesley reported from Quebec and the Maritimes.

TERRY MILEWSKI grew up in Wales and began reporting for London's *Evening Standard* at the age of seventeen. He moved to Canada in 1972 to work for CKWL — the Cariboo radio network — in Williams Lake, British Columbia. Later he joined ITV in Edmonton and then CBC-Calgary. He moved to *The National* in 1980 and has been based in Toronto, Ottawa, Jerusalem, and currently, Washington.

ANDY MOIR started as a reporter and editor for the *Brandon Sun* and Halifax's *Fourth Estate*. For two years, he co-hosted for CBC-Radio's morning show in Winnipeg. In 1978, he became senior producer for CBC-Radio's *Sunday Morning*. In 1981, he moved to *The Journal* as senior editor. Since 1989, he has been the CTV *National News* senior news editor.

JASON MOSCOVITZ moved from his native Montreal after university to become reporter, anchor, and producer of the evening news for North Bay's CTV affiliate, CKNY. Later, he went on to CBMT, Montreal's CBC affiliate, and reported on Quebec's National Assembly for three years. He moved to Ottawa and *The National* in 1980 and reported on national affairs for eight years. He is now the national affairs correspondent for CBC-Radio news.

KNOWLTON NASH began his journalism career as a reporter for *The Globe and Mail*, Toronto, in the mid-1940s. In 1956, Nash began reporting on Washington affairs for CBC-Radio and CBC-TV. He was appointed chief correspondent and anchor of *The National* in 1978, a job he performed for ten years. Now, as senior correspondent, Nash is anchor of *Saturday Report*, anchors the Friday and Saturday editions of *The National*, and produces documentaries for *The Journal*.

DON NEWMAN has spent more than half his twenty years as a broadcast journalist reporting from Parliament Hill. A native of Winnipeg, he has been CBC's national reporter in western Canada and Washington, as well as Washington bureau chief for CTV. Newman appears on CBC's News Specials' coverage of federal elections, federal party conventions, budget broadcasts, and First Ministers' meetings.

CRAIG OLIVER was born in Vancouver and he began his long career in broadcasting as a reporter in Prince Rupert, British Columbia, for the local CBC station. He worked for CBC's *The National* for fifteen years, then moved to CTV to become the first producer of *Canada* AM. Later he served as CTV's Washington bureau chief, doing regular reports from Central America — a place he is now reluctant to send anyone else. He is currently CTV's Ottawa bureau chief.

PHIL PENDRY was born in London, England. As a member of the British Forces, he served as an investigative photographer at the Nuremberg trials. He became a free-lance cameraman for the CBC in the early fifties, based in London, Tokyo, and Paris. In twenty years of service, he covered approximately forty wars. He is currently an independent cameraman.

HARRY PHILLIPS worked for ten years as an all-purpose news reader/light-bulb changer at CKNW radio in his native Vancouver. He served two years as a reporter for CBC-TV's Vancouver supper-hour show. Since 1984, he has been a documentary producer for *The Journal*.

MARK PHILLIPS left his native Montreal to become a parliamentary reporter for the CBC *National News* in 1976. He became the CBC's London correspondent in 1980. He was hired by CBS *News* in 1982 and has reported for that network from London, Moscow, Rome, and, currently, Washington.

JIM REED directed and produced radio at CKNX in Wingham, Ontario, before he joined CBC in Toronto as a public-affairs studio director in the early sixties. Between 1962 and 1972, he was a free-lance working out of Canada and Latin America for *The New York Times*, CBS, *The Boston Globe*, and Associated Press. In 1972, he joined CTV's *W5* as a producer and became a host in 1978.

SUSAN REISLER was an Ottawa-based reporter for United Press International from 1971 to 1976. She then joined CBC Radio *National News* as an editor and later *Sunday Morning* as a reporter. In 1981 she was appointed CBC Radio News correspondent in Washington. She joined *The Journal* in 1981.

LLOYD ROBERTSON's broadcasting career began in 1951 when he signed up with CJCS Radio in his home town of Stratford, Ontario. He moved to CBC *Weekend News* in Toronto in 1962 and in 1970 joined CBC's *The National*, a program he anchored for six years. In 1976 he was hired by CTV National News as co-anchor. He became chief anchor and senior news editor in 1983.

EVE SAVORY was born in Duncan, British Columbia, and began her journalism career in 1973 as an on-the-street radio interviewer for CHQM in Vancouver. Her television career began with CBOT — Ottawa's local CBC station. In 1979, she moved to *The National*, reporting from Regina, Edmonton, and now, Toronto, where she is the medicine and science specialist.

DOUG SMALL was born in Gull Lake, Saskatchewan. From 1970 to 1975, he was an editor and reporter with Canadian Press. He spent one year, 1975, working as director of information for the Food Prices Review Board and the Anti-inflation Board. He returned to journalism with Canadian Press as senior political writer. From 1979 to 1980, he was a columnist and editor of the FP news service. He became Ottawa bureau chief for Global television news in 1980.

ALISON SMITH was born in Osoyoos, British Columbia. She started her reporting career with CBLT in Toronto in 1977. She moved to *The National* in 1982 as a Toronto-based national correspondent. In 1988, she became domestic assignment editor. Currently, in addition to occasionally anchoring *The National*, she hosts Newsworld's *This Day*.

BRIAN STEWART was born in Montreal and raised in Quebec, Halifax, and England. He launched his career as a local reporter for *The Oshawa Times*, spent two years at *The Richmond Times* in England, and landed at *The Gazette* in Montreal in 1968. In 1972, he became host of Montreal's current-affairs show *Hourglass*. He moved to Ottawa and the CBC *National News* in 1974, and served as a parliamentary correspondent. In 1982, he became a foreign correspondent based in London, with responsibilities for Europe, Africa, and the Middle East. In late 1985, he moved to the American network NBC, where he stayed until 1987. He is now a writer and a regular contributor to the CBC's *The Journal*.

LORRAINE THOMSON's thirty years of broadcasting experience include early years as a television dance choreographer and eighteen years as a producer with *Front Page Challenge*.

PAMELA WALLIN was born and raised in Wadena, Saskatchewan. After a stint as a social worker at the Prince Albert Penitentiary, Wallin became co-host of a noon-hour, open-line show on CBC-Radio Regina in 1972. Later, she worked for CBC-Radio's *Sunday Morning* and *As It Happens* out of Ottawa and Toronto. After two years as a reporter for *The Toronto Star*, she joined CTV in 1981 as the Ottawa-based host for *Canada* AM. Currently she is national-affairs correspondent and weekend anchor for CTV *National News*, and moderator of CTV's weekly *Question Period*.